The Yoginî Temples of India

In the pursuit of a mystery
Travel notes

The Yoginî Temples of India

In the pursuit of a mystery
Travel notes

Stella Dupuis

PILGRIMS PUBLISHING
◆ Varanasi ◆

The Yoginî Temples of India
In the pursuit of a mystery
Travel notes
by
Stella Dupuis

Published by:
PILGRIMS PUBLISHING

An imprint of:
PILGRIMS BOOK HOUSE

B 27/98 A-8, Nawabganj Road
Durga Kund, Varanasi-221010, India
Tel: 91-542-2314060
Fax: 91-542-2312456
E-mail: pilgrims@satyam.net.in
Website: www.pilgrimsbooks.com

Illustrations by Edmundo Moure E.
Photos by Stella Dupuis

Edited by Christopher N Burchett
Cover Design & Layout by Roohi Burchett

ISBN: 978-81-7769-665-3
ISBN: 81-7769-665-3

Printed in India at Pilgrim Press Pvt. Ltd. Lalpur, Varanasi.

CONTENTS

Invocation..7

Introductory note...9

Preface..18

Two Yoginî Temples in Orissa..............................20

1.Hirapur temple...27

2.Ranipur Jharial temple..33

The Kingdom of Kalachuri-Chedi...........................38

3.Shahdol site..41

4.Bheraghat temple..45

The Territory of the Chandella Kings.....................50

5.Khajuraho temple..53

6.Dudhai temple..58

7.Badoh site..62

8.Mitauli temple..65

9.Naresar site..69

10.Lokhari site..72

11.Rikhiyan site...76

12.Varanasi..81

13.Hinglajgarh site...84

14.Kanchipuram..87

15.Delhi – Yoginîpura..90

16.Guwahati...92

17.Kathmandu..96

Museums...100

Itineraries...104

Select bibliography..116

I invoke the God Bhairava in all his forms
I invoke His companions the Yoginîs
For their laughter and dances
For their Creation and Recreation

To Matsyendranâtha, omnipresent Guru and Siddha

For Ruben, Nora and Malik, visitors from many lives
May the wings on their feet bring them to the Yoginîs
May they learn to dance within the Divine

To Richard for his loving support
To O.P. Jain founder of Sanskriti Kendra, oasis of serenity and creativity
To Devangana Desai for her generosity and intelligence
To Vidhya Dehejia for her fabulous book about the Yoginîs
To Steve Small, a luminous bridge to the Infinite

To all those who helped me in my travels
particularly the drivers
Ajay Tripathi, Teeja Singh, Dilip Mohanty and Devaraj D. Bala

Note

Sometimes I feel that I was captivated by India from even before birth. Yoga began the dialogue between the wisdom of an ancient civilization and my baggage as a woman of Latin America. Intuitively, I imagined that behind the sophisticated Indian philosophic system there existed a number of beliefs, rites and colourful legends and traditions similar to those of in my native Panama.

For more than twenty-five years I have explored the vast subcontinent that is India. Nevertheless, it was not until the spring of 2005 that I heard of the temples of the Yoginîs.

In the outskirts of Bhubaneshwar, in the state of Orissa, I discovered one of the most fascinating places of India: the temple of the Sixty-four Yoginîs of Hirapur. The experience I lived there was extraordinary; similar in intensity to that which I experienced many years earlier, accompanied by my sons, in the temple of Kâmâkhya[1], near Gawhati. Even today, twenty years later, when I bring up with them what happened during the Puja to the Great Goddess there, words vanish and our silence is a smile in honor of its mystery.

In the temple of the "Sixty-Four Yoginîs" of Hirapur I passed beyond the experience of the bliss of the senses and all understanding. After contemplating one of the figures of the Yoginîs, my eyes closed and my body folded into a sitting position. I remained seated at the feet of the first Yoginî to the left of the entrance. Silence filled the stone shell of the temple beneath the open sky. Distantly, more and more distantly, the world continued

---

[1] Shaktapita = temple dedicated to the Devi, represented by a stone with the Yoni (Vulva) form.

to turn while my soul expanded in the primordial waters of devotion. I returned to the experience of the senses upon feeling myself wrapped by a fresh breeze. Many dragonflies fluttered happily above my head. I felt that they passed through my body as if I were ethereal. The light of sunset transformed their wings into vibrant iridescent filigrees. Smiling, without thinking of anything else, I returned to meditation.

Time stood still until I heard the impatient voice of my friend and travel companion repeating my name. It was getting late; she was tired and wanted to return to Bhubaneshwar. I had no desire to do anything in particular. I was serenely happy. Perhaps I might have preferred to remain there to do yoga and meditate within the temple or on an exterior platform on the shore of the pond.

The absence of erotic figures within and on the outside of the temple intrigued me because I had arrived there seeking a tantric sanctuary. I had imagined beautiful friezes in the style of Khajuraho or Konark. I also imagined the walls filled with images of couples copulating and in erotic positions never seen before. The famous magic rites that were celebrated there and the mysterious sexual practices accompanied by captivating experiences intrigued me. But after what I had experienced in meditation, I felt respect and reverence for the desire of those devotees to maintain their rituals and doctrines secret and accessible only to initiates.

Something special had happened to me in that place. I felt a perfect alertness of the senses. My mind was sharper than ever I remember. In the absence of a Master[2] to help me to understand I invoked the proper Yoginîs, ballerinas of the air and Mistresses of the Universe, to guide my footsteps and open the door of intuition. In the days that followed my body reacted violently as if a great cleansing was occurring in each cell of my being, leaving me almost dehydrated. I was unable to retain even a sip of water, and the only thing I wanted was to shower constantly. For two days I let water and more water fall on my body until, on the third

[2] A Master (Guru) is the fundamental requirement to advance in the knowledge of a secret doctrine

day, I could take some in. Instinctively, I sought the nourishment of the water from green coconuts. On the following nights I had dreams I still remember. In one of them, a great round fish swallowed me and I swam about within it observing its veins and arteries that crisscrossed and lost themselves in the walls of the globe that seemed to be its stomach. Hearing the distinct rhythms with which the blood coursed, I learned to discern where that which I knew to be the essence of life flowed; something like bubbles of oxygen. In the other dream, when I went to place a straw to drink from the hole in a green coconut, it was as if I were pulled within it, although my hands continued to hold the coconut – as if I were both within and outside the coconut at the same time. I felt that although I was outside I had to shake the coconut to free the person that was inside – who was also me – and who had no desire to come out or remain within; I simply let myself be taken by the waves of movement of the water inside.

Logically, both dreams insinuated themselves into my intellect, which was eager for a rational structure, and which had lived some kind of rite of initiation. There came to my mind the writings of Mircea Eliade on Initiations, Rites and Symbols and on the Sacred and the Profane. I remembered phrases that spoke of the religious man and *"his desire to locate himself in a center"* where there existed the possibility of communication with the Gods. *"The initiation is the first step towards spiritual maturity. In the religious history of humanity we continually find this theme: the initiate, he who has known the mysteries, is he who possesses wisdom."* In effect, I had the sensation of having had a revelation but I was unable to decipher the knowledge I felt vibrating within me. [3]

Thus began my pilgrimage to the Yoginîs. I have let the energy flow. I have given myself over to the guidance and the protection of the Yoginîs. I have unexpectedly discovered myself start on routes with no apparent connection between them. Looking from a distance, where I went to Peru to seek information for a novel,

[3] Diary, February 23, 2005.

11

the mystery of the Nazca propelled me again to India. I heard echoes of rites that I imagined were carried out in the grooves of the Nazca drawings but the notes I made hinted at the Yoginîs and not at the ancient inhabitants of the Nazca. The novel I was prepared to write in Peru began to disappear and my mind remained free to perceive clearly the road toward the fiction novel on the Yoginîs and their religion.

I needed more information. It was not easy to prepare the trip to the land of the Goddesses. A veil of mystery lies over the name of the Yoginîs. Their temples or sculptural presence is not mentioned in historical texts or those on sacred architecture, nor in those on religious iconography. After exploring an innumerable number of libraries in Delhi I found two books: *Yoginîs Shrines and Saktipithas* from the collection *Indian Gods and Godesses*, volume 4 of Shantilal Nagar, 2006, B. R. Publishing Corporation, and *Yoginî Cult and Temples, A Tantric Tradition* of Vidya Dehejia, 1986, National Museum, New Delhi[4]. The latter I consider a treasure and was the reward for my efforts. It is a study of the cult sites and their sculptures based on a systematic, comparative and minute analysis of ancient and modern texts. In addition to possessing a profound knowledge of the different eras of the history of Indian art, Dr. Dehejira is a master of the art of deduction and possesses the gift of being able to share her knowledge.

As an introduction to the theme of the cult of the Yoginîs, I wish to cite extracts from the prologue to the book "The Sacred and the Profane" of Mircea Eliade, with the hope of communicating to the reader the same respect and admiration which her words stimulated in me. "…*To present, in two hundred pages, in an understandable and pleasant form, the behavior of **homo religiosus,** is not possible without running risks; in the first place, because of the situation of man in traditional and oriental societies. The spirit that motivates us to provide access to the theme might be interpreted as the expression of a secret*

---

[4] Sold only in the library of the National Museum of Delhi.

*nostalgia for the obsolete condition of archaic **homo religiosus,** which is an attitude completely foreign to this writer. Our intention has been that of helping the reader perceive not only the profound significance of a religious existence of an archaic and traditional kind, but also to help him recognize its validity as a human decision; to appreciate its beauty, its 'nobility.'…*

…. We wish to demonstrate something more: the logic and grandeur of its concepts of the World, i.e., of its conduct, its symbolisms and its religious systems. When one wishes to understand a strange behavior or a system of exotic values, demystifying them does nothing…. It is in the extent to which we accept this belief that we understand its symbolism…"

Alexandra David Neel[5], Giuseppe Tucci[6], Mircea Eliade[7], Pierre Loti[8] and others opened the road to the East for the modern western traveler. India and its mysteries attract millions of tourists. The cultural adventure is revealed to the visitor. The poly-chromatic exoticism, the geography, the beaches, the oceans and rivers captivate the cameras. Art, folklore and spirituality mingle with the names of exotic gods. Definitions of new concepts are added to the lexicon of the traveler. In its dizzy unfolding, India opens its doors and gives welcome to the visitor. Five star hotels proliferate everywhere. Millions of eyes simultaneously admire the Taj Mahal, the palaces in Rajasthan and the beaches or Ayurvedic centers in southern India.

The territory is immense and full of immense contrasts. Millions of people of diverse languages and culture live together in India. I have always marveled at the small arrogance hidden behind the

---

[5] Alexandra David Neel, 1868-1969, of French and Belgian nationality, was the first European to visit Lassa. A great orientalist, historian, adventurer and scholar.

[6] Giuseppe Tucci, 1894-1984, Italian, linguist and historian of ancient cultures.

[7] Mircea Eliade, 1907-1986, Rumanian, famous historian of religion.

[8] Officer of the French navy, great traveller and author. His real name was Louis Marie Julien Viaud, (1850-1923).

French expression "J'ai fait l'Inde." (I've done India) with which some travelers summarize their vacations in India. Tourists don't "do" India. On the contrary, India "does" us. It builds us; it helps us discover unexplored facets of our personality by confronting us with innumerable unexpected situations.

Even for India's own inhabitants the country is difficult to know, either because of its breadth or because of the prolific creativity which characterizes them always and in all fields: art, folklore, languages, philosophy, spirituality, etc.

The philosophic and religious movement that unfolded around the temples of the Yoginîs is little known, given that it was buried under a large number of prejudices. It belongs to the spiritual current known as Tantra[9]. Between the 6th and 12th centuries, tantra spread and interpenetrated all the vernacular religions and all the castes of India. This represented a great victory for the lower classes who had preserved their beliefs and mysteries through the oral tradition[10]. "…It is through this path (the tantra) that the great underground current of autochthonous and native spirituality comes to Hinduism."[11]

It is not an easy undertaking to present the origin and cult of a divinity in a clear and structured manner within the elaborate, complex and varying religious system of medieval times in the Indian subcontinent. The matter becomes even more difficult when what we try to undertake an esoteric cult dedicated to the worship of groups of feminine deities such as the Yoginîs.

In the tantric doctrines, all that which is the source of life is sacred; for that reason the body and human sensibility serve as vehicles for achieving transcendence.

---

[9] Tantra is a system in which the female energy appears as the holder of the keys and explanations for the rhythms of the mysteries of creation and dissolution.

[10] The vernacular cults seem have been devoted to a Mother Goddesses before the arrival of male Gods with the Arians. Commented by Mircea Eliade; Le Yoga, Inmortalité et Liberté

[11] Mircea Eliade, Le Yoga, Immortalité et Liberté, p. 207.

Note

One day when I didn't feel like doing sâdhana[12], I tried to excuse my laziness by claiming I had an unpleasant sensation in my body. My Master replied:

"The Devas are jealous of you."

"Jealous?" I replied, laughing. "Of what? If they are celestial and I a mere mortal…"

"Your body with its functions are the vehicle for reaching the state they yearn for. With meditation and your practices you transcend all that surrounds you; you experience the state where nothing bothers you, where you are completely free. They don't have a body…they do not know this experience…they do not know the 'absolute.' "

"The Devas are jealous of my body?" I added, unbelieving.

"Your body is here and now, it is the 'living rite.' The cosmos is found within your body. Your body is the Temple of all possibilities. Through it you discover the extreme subtlety of the senses. Its functions contain the rhythms of creation. Discipline and the asanas[13] and the rhythms of the breath teach you to control the temporal and how to transcend it, to become timeless, where there are no bonds. Where you are completely free."

Yoga and Tantra are intimately connected. Some texts speak of Matsyendranathâ as the Adi Nâtha, the perfect expression of Lord Shiva, who is the father of Yoga. They also speak of Master Matsyendrnâtha as the father of the trantric religion in which a group of goddesses called the Yoginîs were worshipped.

Often the cult of the Yoginîs was identified as the cult of the "sixty-four Yoginîs", but there also exist temples dedicated to forty-two and eighty-one Yoginîs. The temples are found in the center and northeast of India – in the states of Orissa, Madya Pradesh, Uttar Pradesh – and some sculptures have also been found in the state of Tamil Nadu. The Yoginîs are changing divinities. Each temple has its Yoginîs with diverse characteristics. There is no uniformity in the iconography and each group of Yoginîs appears to have its own identity.

---

[12] Sâdhana = practices with spiritual goals.
[13] Asanas = Postures (Yoga).

Until now the only known text that presents the religious practices related to the religion of the Yoginîs is the Mahâ-Kauljñânanirnaya. Some historians suggest that sexual practices and bloody sacrifices were carried out in the temples. This interpretation is based on the literal readings of the tantric texts (such as the Mahâ-Kauljñânanirnaya) and in the fearful characteristics of some Yoginî sculptures without considering the "symbolic language" factor. Sometimes I find it difficult to understand this point of view inasmuch as the iconography of all the divinities of the Indian pantheon is filled with symbolisms and also because it is widely known that the tantras were written in a purely symbolic language.

The body is one of the mediums used in spiritual practices influenced by Yoga and Tantra. I suspect that the iconography of the goddesses also must have played an important role in the sâdhana that was carried out in the temples of the Yoginîs. Through the image of the divinity the adept left of his mental universe and penetrated the Universe of the deity; he would experience the deity's strength and his attributes expressed in a symbolic language. (Many of the Yoginîs have the heads of animals[14] and the body of a woman[15]). Perhaps the experience would bring about an exchange of energy. We may suppose that first the adept mentally gave over his own body to the Goddess to give her access to the extreme sensory experience until she- through the body of the devotee- reached the most refined limit of perception. Later, the Goddess might transcend the sensory universe and experience the "Absolute". If we develop my Master's thought, the Yoginîs – as spiritual entities – would exist in the manifest World and would be refined divine expressions, but who would not know the "Absolute." If indeed the human being would need the Yoginîs in order to acquire powers that only they knew how to obtain (the techniques of the siddhis), these goddesses would be happy to

[14] Probably, like in many other cultures the strength and characteristics of the animal played an important roll

[15] Symbol of creation; from where all possibilities can be born

16

effect an exchange. For that it would be necessary that the sadhaka[16] to give himself with devotion, abandoning his fears and prejudices.

Given that this deals with an impenetrable doctrine which only transmitted knowledge orally to initiates, we have at our disposition very little direct information, and any interpretation is speculative.

The Yoginî temples are found in isolated places. Doctor Dehejira – who is an authority in this matter – was of the opinion in her book on the Yoginîs that the temples were constructed away from the cities in order to prevent the practices from being seen by intruders because they were of rough character. Personally, I think that the devotees merely sought silence and peace in order to achieve their own spiritual sadhana. I can even imagine that those same adepts of the cult spread the stories of the macabre power of the Yoginîs so that the curious and the uninitiated would not come near the temples.

The fascination of the Yoginîs still lives within the coded verses of the sacred texts, hidden in the legends and in the images of the Goddesses and in their temples. With invisible sacred threads the pilgrim weaves his own fascinating interpretation in which the Yoginîs will appear as protectors, spiritual guides and accomplices in the experience of life.

---

[16] The disciple, practitioner.

Preface

In all the East there yet exists the concept
that a book should not reveal things;
a book should simply help us discover them.

Jorge Luis Borges

To help the reader familiarize himself with the enigmatic themes related to the religion of the Yoginîs and their temples, I offer three books:

1. **The translation of the original manuscript of the** *Mahâ-Kaulajñânanirnaya[17]*, written on palm leaves in a coded language. This work is attributed to the school of the Master *Matsyendranâtha*, a text which treats of the adoration of the Yoginîs. Matsyendrnâtha is also the father of Yoga and the founder of the spiritual discipline of the Yoginî-Kaula in which the energy of the Yoginîs is primordial in the path of the spirit.

2. **Novel: In the Belly of the Fish.** Through fiction, I begin a voyage to an encounter with the fascinating world of *Matsyendranâtha*, who broke away from the ideas of established religions. To him is attributed the doctrine in which a distinct group of Yoginîs was worshipped. With the liberty permitted by a novel, I will weave a narration between historical facts, mysteries and legends. As previously mentioned, we have no direct information on the cult of the Yoginîs. The conjectures to which I have arrived on their practices and doctrine can only be part of an imaginary

---

[1] *Mahâ-Kaulajñânanirnaya* = Esoteric tantric text written in Gupata-Newar characters, of the 11th (?) century. This manuscript was found at the beginning of the 20th century in the royal library of Katmandu. This text mentions the doctrine of the cult of the Yoginîs while in other Tantras we only find lists of the names of the Yoginîs.

tale, in which Master *Matsyendranâtha* appears as the perfect reflection of the great God *Shiva* when he takes on the form of *Bhairava* – the protecting lord of the path of initiates.

3. **Thematic Guide**: A description of the temples of the sixty-four, forty-two and eighty-one Yoginîs, and the best way to arrive at them. Also given is the location of sculptures that are no longer found at their site of origin. The itineraries cover geographic zones and the time necessary to travel them. Since we do not have the exact historical data on the construction of the temples, their patrons or the practices that were carried out there, the book makes reference to legends and esoteric texts and manuscripts that speak of the Yoginîs.

One week itinerary: The temples and sculptures that are in their site of origin: Hirapur, Ranipur, Jharial and Bheraghat.

Two weeks: To those temples mentioned above are added those of Khajuraho, Mitauli and Dudhai[18]; nearby museums are also named where sculptures can be located.

Three weeks: To the listing of the temples and museums of Orissa, Madhya Pradesh and Uttar Pradesh, a trip to the city of Varanasi is also included due to its legends about the Yoginîs.

Complete itinerary: Here are included the sites of Hinglajgadh (at the border between Madhya Pradesh and Rajasthan) and Kanchipuram outside Chennai. It also mentions Guwahati, Delhi and Katmandu as cities related to the cult of the Yoginîs.

---

[18] These temples are found empty.

TWO YOGINÎ TEMPLES IN ORISSA

(Hirapur and Ranipur Jharial)

Accurate data about the cult of the Yoginîs does not exist. As a result, one is constantly forced to employ adverbs such as *probably, eventually,* and *maybe.* The clues studied to understand the mysterious appearance of this group of goddesses reveal that their conception unfolded within a well-structured and refined religious doctrine, influenced by indigenous cults and by orthodox religions that spread through Orissa during a particular period of time.

Two of the oldest temples dedicated to the Yoginîs can be found in Orissa. To understand their historical and religious context, an overview of the region's history is necessary.

The first known inhabitants of Orissa were the Kalingas, who were praised for their strength and courage while defending their territory against the powerful army of King Ashoka. It is said that Ashoka was so shocked by the resulting massacre that he began to study the teachings of Buddha. This episode was deeply engraved in Indian history because it led to that famous king converting to Buddhism in 262 B.C.E., two years after the tragedy.

No proof exists that a Brahmin–Vedic faith had developed in pre-Buddhist Orissa. The Jains arrived at a later date (the Udayagiri and Khandagiri caves near Bhubaneshwar are testimony to this) when they began to have an impact on the religious landscape of the region. It is also said that Adi Shankar[19] sent one of his four disciples to Puri to establish Hinduism there. From that time, a refined architectural style began to flourish in the religious centres

---

[19] Adi Shankar = Philosopher and reformer of Indic religions. A variety of traditions and legends say that he lived around the 2nd or 3rd centuries, but historians place him in the 8th century.

of Orissa with the construction of the extraordinary temples that can still be seen in Bhubaneshwar, Konark and Puri.

Although the larger religious trends were welcomed in Orissa, their practices differed from those of other areas because they blended with the existing beliefs of the different vernacular ethnic populations. Many tribes still exist today that have managed to preserve their identities and customs.

From time immemorial in almost every culture in the world the concept of a goddess has been tied to the themes of maternity and fertility, and is therefore a symbol of prosperity and power. The iconography of the Devi in the different indigenous sects of India did not emphasize maternal love as it did in the west, but rather the essence of protection: the power to destroy evil. In Orissa there are countless rural temples dedicated to the Devi, who is identified with the earth, the mountains or the jungle, and who is worshipped with offerings of coconuts wrapped in red cloth[20] hung on branches or on small altars that decorate the sides of the roads and pathways. These offerings also appear in the wild forest, in temples decorated with drawings and bas-reliefs that demonstrate how much imagination and care were applied in expressing the iconography of the goddess – an all powerful female being.

It is reasonable to conclude that the Yoginî cult was welcomed in Orissa because its inhabitants were prepared to worship a pantheon of goddesses of which they were intuitively aware. It is also probable that the sect's followers spread macabre legends about the Yoginîs in order to preserve their privacy. The temples were deliberately constructed in remote locations. Today, when the sky turns toward sunset the visitors and locals quickly abandon the Yoginî shrines. The fear promulgated by the esoteric

---

[20] The color red is identified with the Devi. It also symbolizes secret knowledge, the vital mystery of the blood which flows hidden within the body. When a man bleeds it is because he is wounded and may die, while the woman survives each month the "shedding" of her blood. The coconut is also a feminine symbol, the womb where the primordial waters are housed.

cults and by the spells attributed to various manifestations of those powerful deities continues to exist even to this day. In the mind of the non-initiated, the shadows of the night stir the Yoginîs' blood-lust, causing them to possess or devour the first human who crosses their path.

The Yoginîs probably came to be worshipped through a tribal religion, retaining their ogre aspect in order to frighten away evil forces[21] while also bringing their peaceful nature in order to attract beneficial influences.

Legends about the arrival of the Yoginîs into the pantheon of the Sixty-Four gods can be found in indigenous lore. Some legends speak of them as an emanation of Durga, assistants in the battle against an evil personified by powerful demons. In others they appear as women who acquired divine powers through magic or through devotion to Durga, Shiva or Bhairava. They are also referred to as the eight multiplications of the eight Mothers (the seven *Sapta Mâtrikâs*[22] to which *Yogeshvarî*[23] is added to make an eighth). These mothers are in turn the feminine counterparts of the ancient Vedic gods *Kubera, Yama, Varuna*, etc. (the goddesses have the same name as the god but the last letter "a" is changed to an "i"), or they originate from a more recent pantheon such as *Mâhêshvara (Shiva), Brahma, Vishnu, Kumâra*, etc. This most recent iconography of the seven mother goddesses is composed of: *Brahmânî, Mâhêshvari, Kaumârî, Vaishnâvi, Vârâhi, Indrâni* and *Châmundâ*.[24] The spelling varies from one text to another.

---

[21] In "evil" we include the fear that paralyzes the mind. Fear is one of the most unfortunate of human emotions.

[22] Sapta Mâtrikâs = The group of the seven mother goddesses. They are found portrayed in innumerable temples. Châmundâ is one of the Sapta Mâtrikâs although her iconography is fearsome and not one of a gentle mother. Châmundâ appears as an emanation of Durga when she had to destroy the demons Chânda and Mundâ. When Yogeshwari is added to the Sapta Mâtrikâs, the group is said to be the Ashta Mâtrikâs. (Eight Mothers).

[23] Yogeshwari = Feminine counterpart of Shiva in his form of Yogeshwara, God of Yoga. Yogeshwari is recognizable by the third eye on her forehead.

[24] Generally, the Mâtrikâs are portrayed in a sitting position.

While it seems that Orissa was not influenced by the *Mâtrikâs* of the Vedic period, they must have arrived through the influx of the *shakta*[25] and *tántric*[26] cults and ideas that appeared simultaneously with the traditional religions. The worship of the *Sapta Mâtrikâs* found fertile ground in Orissa. Various temples constructed there during the 9th and 10th centuries A.D. were dedicated exclusively to them. This might be the reason why the ensemble of Yoginîs in the temples at Hirapur and Ranipur Jharial – constructed during the same period – lacked the Mâtrikâs. In the temples of that period the Mâtrikâs were portrayed seated in the *lalita asana*[27] position in which the goddess has one leg tucked in and the other extending downwards to rest on a lotus flower or an animal. This is the pose in which gods or kings were portrayed, and sculpturing the Yoginîs in such a pose gave them the status of goddesses. However, the Yoginîs of Hirapur and Ranipur Jharial are sculpted in a standing position.

The Orissa temples raise a number of questions. Starting from the fact that the temple in Ranipur Jharial is the oldest remnant of the Yoginî cult, the theory that the Yoginîs are the eight Matrikas multiplied by eight characteristics does not comport with the Orissa Yoginîs because they are not portrayed in the same form as the Matrikas. If the indigenous tribal deities were the only influence the pantheon of the Yoginîs, the images and details would be simplistic or archaic but instead they are the expressions of complex esoteric and abstract concepts. The question then arises: Where did the Yoginîs come from? Where the number of sixty-four female deities come from? Where did the doctrine of the cult of the sixty-four Yoginîs originate?

[25] Shaktas = Generally written in the Roman alphabet with SH. The Saktas or Shaktas would be the worshippers of the divine feminine energy (Shakti), the complement to the divine masculine energy.

[26] Tantra = Great esoteric and mystical tradition requiring the assistance of a master. Sacred texts written in code which seek to awaken the divine energy within the body in order to raise consciousness to more refined levels.

[27] This posture indicates that the character represented is of elevated status. (A god or king).

While in the states of Madhya Pradesh and Uttar Pradesh both circular and rectangular temples are found containing sixty-five[28], sixty-seven[29], forty-two[30] and eighty-one[31] Yoginîs (which apparently included in their traditions the Mâtrikâs), the only two temples in Orissa are round and both contain sixty-four Yoginîs, in a tradition that did not include the Mâtrikâs.

Thus, the Yoginî cult in Orissa probably arose out of Tantric currents that flourished in Bengala and Assam to the north of Orissa and nearby. In fact, the esoteric doctrine of the Yoginîs is attributed to the great master Matsyendrnâtha who apparently was born east of the Gulf of Bengal in what is today Bangladesh. It is also said that the revelation of the Yoginî cult occurred to Matsyendrnâtha in Kâmarupa (in the state of Assam).

Set forth below is an extract of the *Mahâ-Kauljñananirnaya* in which the school of Matsyendranâtha expounds upon the power of the eight forms of knowledge, each expressed in eight different ways.

… Now listen to the eight Vidyâs: Hrîm Ksah, Hrîm Lah, Hrîm Hah, Hrîm Sah, Hrîm Va, Hrîm Ra[32]. The parts of the Vidyâ[33] are eightfold. Hrîm Klhrîm is Kaulika Bhairavi[34]. One should combine the Vidyâ (knowledge) in eight ways. The first of the eight has been spoken. Just as this has been formed in

---

[28] The Mitauli temple has sixty-five niches; there probably was a tutelary goddess there who presided over the group of sixty-four Yoginîs.

[29] The Khajuraho temple has sixty-seven niches, one of greater size being for the tutelary goddess and the other two probably housing the goddesses of the Yamuna and Ganga Rivers which were deeply venerated in the region.

[30] The temples of Dudhai and Badoh held forty-two Yoginîs.

[31] The temple of Bheraghat has eighty-one Yoginîs.

[32] Mantras. It is said that the mantras must be learned only from a master. A mantra without specific instructions for using it properly will not provide the desired results.

[33] Vidyâ = Knowledge.

[34] Kaulika Bhairavi = name of a divinity or a « divine state of consciousness » related with the Kaula schools that worshiped the Yoginîs in a circle where Bhairava was the central axe.

a combination, so all the Yoginîs should be considered as combining in the same way. (Mahâ-Kauljñananirnaya, Patala VIII, 31).

Multiplying eight with eight makes sixty-four Yoginîs according to their due order. The first Chakra gives the power of being one with the Yoginîs, and having the power of minuteness and obtaining the other eight Siddhis – though practice of meditation and sâdhana.[35] Of this there is no doubt... (Mahâ-Kauljñananirnaya, Patala VIII, 32-33).

The orthodox Brahmin schools – established and respected within the monarchies – considered the Tantras a menace and characterized their beliefs as those of inferior castes or of lesser quality. Nevertheless, the temples to the Yoginîs were probably favored by the royalty.

Because nothing is clear regarding this cult, it is difficult to discuss its temples. Until the middle of the 20th century, no book on sacred architecture mentioned the temples of Hirapur and Ranipur Jharial.

Near Hirapur Temple

---

[35] Sadhâna = Techniques.

Rural Temples, Orissa

1. HIRAPUR

(End of 9ᵗʰ Century, early 10ᵗʰ Century)

The Hirapur temple dedicated to the sixty-four female deities known as the Yoginîs is located fifteen kilometers from Bubaneshwar, the capital of the state of Orissa.

As to who financed this open-air, dark-stoned shrine and when it might have been constructed, Dr. Vidya Dehejia[36] suggests it may have been one of the rulers of the Bhañja dynasty, a minor kingdom, who around 900 C.E. extended his reign to the coastal region of Orissa. The motivation to dedicate a specific site for the worship of the Yoginîs often arose out of necessity. Wealthy feudal chieftains,

Hirapur Temple

---

[36] <u>Yoginî Cult and Temples</u>, A Tantric Tradition.

kings or queens sought refuge in such times of crisis as natural disasters, plagues or illnesses, or when it was necessary to overcome an enemy, consolidate territory or achieve new conquests.

The controversy over whether the Yoginîs of Hirapur include the Mâtrikâs[37] is discussed in a variety of commentaries. Other monographs attempt to make the lists of names found in Tantric texts or in the Purânas (ancient stories) coincide with the iconography of the Yoginîs.

Professor Dehejia demonstrates that the conclusions of some historians, anxious to include the Mâtrikâs in the group of Yoginîs of Hirapur, are usually based on a single factor (often dealing with the animal found at their feet) and not on a systematic study of the corresponding iconography. In her commentary she compares the characteristics of the sculptures with the significance of some names appearing in the lists of Yoginîs set out in the ancient texts.

"…it is tempting to identify the single Yoginî accompanied by an elephant with Indrânî [38], who employs such an animal as a steed. But instead of a vajra (lighting bolt), this graceful figure lifts a skull-cup to her lips. She might be the Yoginî Surâpriyâ drinking wine, or Rudhrirapâyinî drinking blood, or Kapâlinî (she with the cup formed of a skull); but she is not Indrâyanî, and thus we are obligated to conclude that there is no Indrâyanî at Hirapur." [39]

Analyzing each sculpture one by one in this manner, Dr. Dehejia points out the two or three possible errors in associating a specific Yoginî with a "Yoginî-Mâtrikâ". In several Yoginî temples in Madhya Pradesh and Uttar Pradesh, the Mâtrikâs are included in the group of Yoginîs.

---

[37] Mâtrikâs = The introductory section on Orissa mentions the Sapta Mátrikás (seven mothers) and the Achta Mâtrikâs (eight mothers) as possible sources of the sixty-four Yoginîs.

[38] Dr. Dehejia uses the names of the goddess Indrânî or Indrâyanî interchangeably. As previously mentioned, the orthography of a god's name may vary even within a single text.

[39] Yoginî Cult and Temples, A Tantric Tradition, Vidya Dehejia, page 97.

Hirapur is the only Yoginî temple in which sculptures exist on the outside of the enclosure. These include nine niches with deities or important female individuals to whom homage is rendered (they are portrayed accompanied by assistants who protect them with parasols, and even today the parasol continues to be a symbol of respect with which the great masters are greeted, regardless of the weather). These sculptures bear a sabre in one hand and a skull-cup in the other. They may fulfil the function of guardians or, being nine in number, relate to the nine goddesses of Navaratri[40]. The number nine is also sacred because the soul of Mahâbhairava [41] is made up of nine elements: (1) the weather in all its forms, (2) material things that exist such as the colour blue, (3) names and their sounds, (4) perception, the five senses, (5) consciousness, (6) heart, (7) desire-will, (8) intelligence and (9) mind. Mahâbhairava is in turn the soul of the Goddess. For that reason the soul of the Goddess is also made up of the nine elements.

Yogini

The circular form of the temple opens outward in a form reminiscent of a Yoni (vulva). Two guards stand at the entrance. The low height of the entry arch forces one to stoop and bow down before entering. On both sides of the small corridor before

---

[40] Navaratri = The celebration in which different facets of the Goddess are celebrated over a period of nine nights.
[41] Mahâbhairava = the great god Bhairava.

reaching the inner circle are two skeletal Vetâlas[42] or Bhairavas with garlands of skulls; at their feet is a procession consisting of a jackal and two men carrying a receptacle made of human skulls[43]. Thereafter one reaches the open area. The circumference contains sixty niches with Yoginîs. In the centre of the main platform is an altar where once stood an image of Shiva that has been stolen. On the sides of the central altar are four Yoginîs and four Bhairavas.

Whoever visits Hirapur will notice the beauty of its sculptures regardless of what analytical conclusion they might reach. The world of the Yoginîs unfolds in a dimension independent of reason, in which imagination and intuition blend with devotion. Although the goddesses represented there are part of a puzzle, which leaves the intellect without satisfactory answers, the visitor will be moved by the beautiful artistry of the sculptures.

Yogini

---

[42] Vetâla = Ghosts, images of skeletal beings portrayed with erections. They are associated with Bhairava. They are found on the doors or sides of altars in the temples of south India.

[43] Dogs, jackals, skulls used as a vessel, ghosts or skeletal gods, all probably formed part of the symbolism that was only comprehensible to initiates and which instilled fear in the curious.

In the traditional temples of India, the idols are found in the shadowy interior of the sanctum sanctorum, while the open-air sanctuaries dedicated to the Yoginîs offer *darshan* (a vision of the deity) within a peaceful refuge overflowing with fresh air and sunshine.

Yoginî

Sixty Four Yoginis Temple
Hirapur, Orissa

2. RANIPUR JHARIAL

(Late 9th century)

The second temple dedicated to the Yoginîs in the State of Orissa is located to the west near the border with the State of Chhattisgarh. The site leaves the impression that the temple of Ranipur Jharial was constructed in an imaginary land and then forgotten.[44]

Far from any urban area, the round temple dedicated to the Yoginîs unobtrusively appears on a rocky elevation girdled by a natural pond. Although its dimensions are nearly twice those of the temple of Hirapur, its structure   blends into the surface of the wind-battered rock hill.

[44] In ancient manuscripts Ranipur Jharial was known as "Soma Tirtha".

Near the sanctuary of the Yoginîs lie the remains of temples dedicated to Buddha, Shiva and Vishnu.

Yoginis Ranipur Jharial

The very symbol of free spirits, at Ranipur Jharial the Yoginîs are today protected behind bars, where they are portrayed in the initial standing position for all traditional dances in India, as if to initiate the aerial movement of the dance. Bars were necessary to protect them because the site is open and – as has been seen in other locations – subject to vandalism.

The first encounter with the Yoginîs of Raipur Jharial may lead one to think that the temple is much older than that of Hirapur. However, it is

34

believed to have been built only a few years earlier, towards the end of the 9th century.

The fading of the Yoginîs' features and the general deterioration suffered by the figures is attributed to the quality of the stone from which they were sculpted, which did not resist weathering by the wind, rain and the searing sun.

Bhairava Shrine in the Sixty-Four Yogini Temple
Ranipur Jharial, Orissa

One way to establish the date of the temple's construction is to compare it with the images of Yoginîs from temples which have a known construction date. In the interior of the country, the sculptures of Yoginîs are more elaborate with halos and personages that accompany and adorn the central figure and its vehicle-symbol. For example, the sculptures found at Shadol are the most recent, dating from the end of the 11th century. It appears that, over the centuries, the codes of beauty required decorating the entire stele. In the upper part, flying nymphs were sculpted on the sides of the

35

halo, and decorations of worshippers or attendants of the goddess placed alongside the central figure and at her feet. In Ranipur Jharial, only the silhouettes of the goddesses arise out of the stone. Often in the iconography of the Yoginîs, the body of a voluptuous woman has the head of an animal, as if to indicate that this detail had a specific meaning for the cult. In the case of Ranipur Jharial, more than a dozen heads of animals – antelopes, horses, buffalos, pigs, elephants, leopards, cats, and others – can be observed.

In the center of the circular temple stands an altar with a three-faced Shiva in position to initiate a dance. Ghanesa and Nandi accompany him at the base of the sculpture. On the other hand, the Yoginis seem to dispense with the need for an acolyte animal figure at their feet, possibly because they themselves personify the symbols of the animal kingdom.

Initially, the entranceway faced south. It was carefully covered over and replaced by an opening facing east. Outside on the large rock are various small temples constructed facing each other. The first of these to be built were most likely those oriented in a north-south direction (relating to the first door of the temple) while farther away are others facing east-west, suggesting that the confrontation of the temple-niches had something to do with the cult's pre-initiation ceremonies.

Although the simplicity of the sculptures aids in dating the temple of Ranipur Jharial at the end of the 9th century, its patrons remain unknown. As stated previously, on the immense rock and in the surrounding area of the Ranipur Jharial temple, ruins of sanctuaries of different sects can be found, but nothing remains of any living quarters. All signs indicate that this serene and isolated site was for many centuries an important center of religious pilgrimage. An inscription in one of the temples on the edge of the pond states that whoever bathed in those sacred waters would be free from sin.

Thirty meters to the west of the temple of Someswar, which is located next to the pond, rises a large rock five meters in height which the locals call the temple of Jogeswar. On this stone the main deity is sculpted facing south[45] and nine Mâtrikâs (mothers) face northeast. The ruins of a mandapa[46] can be distinguished in front of the main deity.

Not far from the sanctuary of the sixty-four Yoginîs lies a ruined temple dedicated to Kamarrja Bhairava.

The solitary site of Raipur Jharial is worth visiting. Each ruin, each sculpture stimulates interest. Walking in the silence of this rocky site, one's eyes open to a new awareness, effortlessly recapturing from the lost past the images of the rites and practices of the Yoginî cult and their sacred environment.

[45] The face of Shiva that faces south is called Bhairava.
[46] Mandapa = pavilion.

THE KINGDOM OF KALACHURI-CHEDI, THE RIVALS OF THE CHANDELLAS

(The Temples of Shahdol and Bheraghat)

As mentioned in the discussion on the temples of Orissa, the temple at Ranipur Jharial seems to be the remains of the oldest temple of the Yoginî cult. This conclusion stems from the fact that the style of the sculptures is simple and only the main figure stands out.

The most recent temples are those at Shahdol[47], to the west of Orissa, given that the style of the Yoginîs there fits with the artistic rules extant at the end of the 11th and 12th centuries. In that period, the principal figures of the Yoginîs were accompanied by detailed stone motifs.

The temples of Shahdol, like that of Bheraghat, are believed to have been built by the rulers of Kalachuri-Chedi, the rivals of the Chandella[48] dynasty. Over the centuries, the Chandellas distinguished themselves by their great power and legacy of sacred architecture. The Chandella constructed temples of a various different of sects along the northern traditional style while creating innovative styles of beauty as it is found in Khajuraho. Also attributed to them are the Yoginî temples of Mitauli, Naresar, Khajuraho, Dudhai, Badoh, Lokhari, Rikhiyan and Hinglajgadh. Neighboring monarchies were awestruck by the proliferation of these temples and these religious symbols were probably sensed as an important reservoir of political power.

One can conjecture that the reason the Kalachuri-Chedi kings constructed the Yoginî temples in their own territory was the belief

---

[47] There are thought to have been two temples in the zone of Shahdol.
[48] The Chandellas were an important dynasty that ruled in central India.

Bheraghat Site

that the Yoginîs were the source of the success of their neighbors. It is also possible that in their pursuit to acquire even more merit than their rivals, these rulers decided to venerate the greatest possible number of Yoginîs; one reason which led them to construct the temple of eighty-one Yoginîs at Bheragat. Finally, some descendants of the patron of Bheraghat financed the dazzling sculptures of the temples at Shahdol.

Although the temples are separated by more than a century, apparently the religion included the Mâtrikâs among the Yoginîs venerated in Bheraghat as well as in the two temples at Shahdol. No evidence exists to indicate that the temples at Shahdol were dedicated to sixty-four Yoginîs or that they continued with the ancestral tradition of venerating eighty-one goddesses, or whether they did so in circular temples or rectangular ones.

In the 10th century the monarchs of Tripura[49] expanded their reign to the west where Bheraghat is located and designated members of their family as viceroys. A century later these earlier

---

[49] An important kingdom of the east.

Achanakmar Forest

envoy became completely independent from the royalty of Tripura, forming their own dynasty.

The Kalachuri and Chedi dynasties – the names by which the kings of the region were known – became allied through matrimonial alliances. Archival have been found concerning a gift of lands – dealing with the religious zone, particularly the tantric region of Amarkantak near Shahdol – which was awarded around the 11th century by one of the kings of the Chedi clan to a member of the Kalachuri clan.

3. SHAHDOL

(11th – 12 Century?)

As the crow flies, the district of Shahdol lies a short distance from Amarkantak and Bheraghat, two sites that are important as they relate to the cult of the Yoginîs and their legends.

During the Middle Ages, arts, ideas and beliefs moved from one place to another despite rugged mountainous terrain making communication between cities difficult. Nonetheless such movement of ideas occurred as if natural barriers did not exist. The cult of the Yoginîs also made its way through mountain ranges like those surrounding the region of Shahdol, surpassing even the Himalayan heights to arrive in Tibet. (Tales of the Yoginîs and Siddhas[50] are found in the magical-religious literature of Tibet). The cult extended even to arid regions and descended to the

Illustration of Srî Vasabhâ,
Yogini from Shahdol,
Original at the
Kolkata (Calcutta) Museum

---

[50] Siddhas = Beings who through certain Yoga techniques as well as others have achieved the goal of life which is to become "in His image and likeness" and thereby come to possess all classes of powers (Siddhis). For the Siddhas, these powers are not "supernatural" but rather "natural" because they belong to the man free from fear and negativity, etc. (A cluster of defects that today we would call "stress").

south of Deccan[51]. Despite such dispersion, a discussion of the temples of the Yoginîs necessarily must refer to the northeastern belt for it is there where the majority of the temples and sculptures of the Yoginîs are found.

Not a single feature remains of the temples that must have existed in the district of Shahdol. Two are mentioned because two sets of sculptures have been found there. In one group the Yoginîs are standing; in the other they are seated. Sculptures in the temples of the Yoginîs usually maintain a uniform posture. (The only exception is that of the goddess Mahisâsurmardinî, for when she kills the bull demon she appears standing over him). The hypothesis that two temples existed in the Shahdol area is also substantiated by the fact that the two styles of Yoginîs found there differ from one another and because two Mahisâsurmardinî were found as well. (No Yoginîs are represented twice in the same temple).

An analysis of the sculptures leads to the conclusion that both temples date from the latter part of the eleventh century, though they came from different workshops. Both types of the Shahdol Yoginîs are richly worked. The central figure is adorned with garlands, bracelets, and amulets, and has many arms. The Yoginîs are also surrounded by assistants and celestial musicians.

To sculpt an image the size of the Shahdol statues with so much detail, an artist today would need at least eight months of intense labor. In that earlier era in which the transportation of the stone blocks was carried out by means of long, narrow carts without sophisticated machinery, the work must have taken about a year. The workshops probably recruited the most talented artists from throughout the territory. And the creation of forty-two, sixty-four and eighty-one Yoginîs must have been stupendously expensive. While the patrons of the traditional temples did not always belong to the royal classes (dedicatory steles have been found which refer to merchants or wealthy landowners), undoubtedly the construction of the Yoginî temples in areas difficult to reach must have been supported by powerful individuals.

[51] Deccan = The plateau between the Eastern and Western Ghat mountains and south of the Vindhya heights.

Inscriptions bearing the names of the Yoginîs are found at their feet. Some refer to goddesses known as Taralâ or Târâni but their vehicles and other characteristics do not match the other Taralâs or Târânis mentioned in some texts or which have been seen in other temples.

Because the tradition of the Yoginî cult was esoteric and transmitted orally, little is known of the ceremonies associated with it. It would appear that some disciples – perhaps facing the threat of Muslim incursions into India – attempted to preserve it by writing down traces of the cult's doctrine into a secret code. Nepal became the center for the preservation of mystical concepts. For a number of centuries, manuscripts were written down in a variety of newari characters that evolved throughout the different time periods. The hermeneutics of the *Srî Matottara Tantra* (known in a simplified version as the Goraksha Samhitâ) and the *Mahâ-Kaulajñânanirnaya* have brought flashes of illumination to the study of the cult. Additionally, the *Srî Matottara Tantra* has a list of the names of the Yoginîs. Other lists are also found in texts where no other reference is made to the Yoginîs. The information reaches us through the meaning of the name because it often makes an allusion to the characteristics of the goddess. When the sculpture contains no inscription with names, historians attempt to find its corresponding name in the lists. (Kâlikâ Purâna, Skanda Purâna, Agni Purâna, Kubjikâpûjâpaddhati, *Srî Matottara Tantra*, and in Jain texts, etc.).

The Yoginîs of Shahdol belong to the tradition in which the Mâtrikâs were included in the circle of Yoginîs. It appears that also included were the feminine counterparts of the Vedic gods who protected the eight cardinal points, these counterparts being called Dikpâlikâs[52].

---

[52] Dikpâlas = Indra, king of the gods, presides over the East; Varuna, god of the oceans, dominates the West; Kubera, god of abundance, reigns over the North; Yama, god of death, deals with roads leading South; Agni, god of fire, rules over the Southwest; Vayu, god of the winds, to the Northwest; Isana (a form of Shiva) rules the Northeast; Nairitya, god of fear, dominates the Southwest.

A few rather deteriorated sculptures were taken to small temples in the towns of Antara and Panchgaon (in the district of Shahdol). Five seated Yoginîs are found in the museum of Kolkata (Calcutta); a standing one appears in the museum of Bhopal, and the others in the museum of Dhubela near Khajuraho.

There is a suggestion that not far from the district of Shahdol, to the north of the Narmada River in the district of Rewa near Gurki, lay a place where a group of goddesses were worshipped, but no concrete evidence exists that a temple to the Yoginîs also stood there.

4. BHERAGHAT

(End of the 10th Century, early 11th Century)

The name of Bheraghat probably derives from the concept of
"Bhairava Ghat"[53] (encounter with Bhairava). Nevertheless, it is
not possible to locate in the temple's circular platform the
impression of the central altar where the idol representing Shiva in
the form of Bhairava would have stood.

Bheraghat Eighty-one Yogini Temple

---

[53] Ghat = Stairs to reach the ritual encounter with the sacred rivers or with
the ocean.

Although the sign at the entrance reads "Chusat Yoginî Temple" (Temple of the Sixty-Four Yoginîs), the sanctuary housed eighty-one Yoginîs, each within an individual niche along the circular wall.

At the beginning of the 20th Century, various manuscripts written on palm sheets were discovered which referred to the cult of the Yoginîs. One manuscript is the *Mahâ-Kaulajñânanirnaya*[54] – which tells in symbolic terms of the cult's practices; the other is the *Sri Mattotara Tantra* which specifies that the circle of eighty-one Yoginîs is particularly advantageous for royalty. The manuscript describes the Mula Chakra in which nine Mâtrikâs (mother goddesses) multiply themselves nine times. As previously mentioned, the group of seven Mâtrikâs[55] is found represented in many temples throughout India (Brahmari, Maheshvari, Kaumari, Vaishnavi, Varahi, Aindri and Châmundâ). Occasionally, eight Mâtrikâs are mentioned in which a Yogeswari is included; and a Mahâlaksmi[56] is included in the Mula Chakra group as the ninth goddess.

A list of Yoginîs is found in the *Sri Mattotara Tantra* but they do not necessarily correspond to the names inscribed in the bases of the blocks of stone where the Yoginîs of Bheraghat are sculptured. Although this temple was used by royalty, it seems that some names of Yoginîs do not come from Sanskrit but rather stem from the traditions of the common folk, as if it was in the hearts of humble people, in the communion with the earth and other elements, where the wisdom and power of the celestial and subterranean worlds was harvested.

---

[54] Alreadey mentioned in pages 11 and 17

[55] Chapter: Two temples dedicated to the Yoginîs in the state of Orissa.

[56] Mahâlakshmi = The great Laksmi, Goddess of wealth, consort of the God Vishnu.

After two hundred years another sanctuary in the traditional style of northern India was constructed within the perimeter of the temple and dedicated, this time, to Shiva. It is difficult to understand why this temple was built completely out of focus. It seems the builders sought to block the fluid movement of the faithful around the great circle. An inscription mentions the queen Gosaladevi and her two sons who in 1190 AD dedicated the temple to Bhanagna Khidra, the "Slayer of Illnesses."

In the temple of Bheraghat only a few of the Yoginîs remain in their original locations. Eight Matricas from an older temple and a Ghanesh were added to the site as if to fill the niches that, for some unknown reason, were left empty.

Practically all the sculptures were vandalized and disfigured. Many lost arms and, logically, the nose. The Muslim invaders were in the habit of removing the noses from the sculptures in order to remove features that symbolized personality. In Islam, as in Judaism, divine images are not permitted nor is the human body to be made into an image. The nose is the essence of the embodied living being. (With the first breath it enters into life and "expires" with the last exhalation). Traditionally, orthodox Hindus do not worship a damaged image – though some accept natural wear – but never an icon damaged by force. The representation of the divine needs to be perfect. However, for the worship by the common folk no restrictive rule exists, and adoration can be expressed before a tree, a rock or a damaged idol. For the soul of the worshipper the divine materializes wherever the heart searches for it. Even today offerings of flowers or food are found daily before the statues of the Yoginîs, whether it is in Bheraghat, Ranipur Jharial or Hirapur.

In Bheraghat only a third of the sculptures survived the vandalism but even so it is possible to enjoy Yoginîs with heads of beasts while the bodies of the women express sensuality by means of their voluptuous figures.

Each of the Yoginîs of Bheraghat dazzles by means of its detail, its multiple arms and seductive body, and through its ornaments and other innumerable details. The decorations that surround the central image on the block of stone are rich in symbolism, making it worthwhile going through the allegorical language.

One of the most impressive sculptures is that bearing the name Kâmadâ, bestower of Love. At its feet can be seen an adoration of the Yoni other (vulva). In the Kâlikâ[57] Purana[58], Kâmadâ,

Fear inspiring yet sensual
Yogini from Bheraghat

Yogini Kâmadâ (detail)

Mahâmâyâ and Kâmâkhyâ are names given to the Devi in verses that exalt the sexual energy (kâma) of the goddess who in her lascivious moments gives blessings and gifts to her devotees.

The eighty-one Yoginîs of Bheraghat were gathered there to protect, to destroy all that might be harmful, and above all to bestow everything that might be necessary to a king and his kingdom.

Lacking any inscription of a date that might shed light directly on the time of the temple's construction, Dr. Dehejia produced an important study of the inscriptions of the names on the pedestals comparing them with the inscriptions in other locations. She also compared the styles of the sculptures, their dates and evidence with corresponding historic periods, etc.

---

[57] Kâlikâ = The aspect of Kâli that controls the weather.
[58] Purana = Spiritual books recounting fables of divine beings and their relationships with man.

Eighty-one Yogini Temple, Bheraghat

She reached the conclusion that the temple must have been built between the years 945 and 1000, during the reign of Yuvaraja II of the Kalachuri dynasty, whose capital lay some seven kilometres from Bheraghat.

THE TERRITORY OF THE CHANDELLA KINGS

Various Tantric sects influenced the religious world of the Chandella dynasty. Of these, the Kaula sects were particularly welcomed among the Chandella kings and possibly even more so by their queens.

The *Mahâ-Kaulajñânanirnaya* of the school of Matsyendrnâtha was apparently one of the secret texts of the Kaula doctrine. A number of the Yoginîs' worship rituals are described in the manuscript in symbolic and metaphoric language, and in chapter XXIII reference is made to the sixty-four Yoginîs.

*Afflicted by planets, **Bhûtas**[59], flame, fire, swords, difficult situations, obstructions, ailments, kings, lightning, tigers, lions or elephants, inspired by various anxiety-producing things from every direction, one may seek the protection of **the sixty-four Yoginîs**. They wander in various forms taking the shapes of various animals. One should never show anger of speech or mind to them, nor should one speak harshly to maidens or women. (Mahâ-Kaulajñânanirnaya, Patala XXIII, 8-11)[60]*

---

[59] Bhûtas = Spirits, beings.

[60] The esoteric traditions were transmitted orally, and often knowledge was transmitted from master to disciple (to make memorization easier sometimes the script took the form of verses and chants where the sound of the words was more important than grammatical construction or the logic of the sentence). The Vedas – which are the most revered texts in Hindu mysticism – were chanted during many centuries before being recorded in written verse. It was during this time that they were most likely adapted to the grammar and refined structure of Sanskrit. Today the Pundits continue to chant the Vedas based on written texts. On the other hand, the Tantra-worshippers always wished to maintain the oral tradition, and if the verses were transcribed this was done through preserving the indigenous language in order to hide spiritual messages within a maze of words.

The followers of the Tantric doctrines subscribed to the interpretations of Masters who probably adapted their knowledge to the needs of the time. The people who built the temples of the forty-two Yoginîs were probably inspired by the mysticism of Sâradâtilaka Tantra, where reference is made to the divine energy of the forty-two letters of the Sanskrit alphabet which should be worshipped as goddesses. The reasons or circumstances that gave rise to this belief remain unknown.

The prosperous and important kingdom of Chandella encompassed the territory between the Jamuna and the Narmada rivers and on the west the Chambal River in what is today Madhya Pradesh. This kingdom was established as an independent power towards the middle of the 10th Century. The selection of the Khajuraho site as a center of religious activity was probably due to its geographic position in the core of what was then the great territory of Chandella. At that time, political power and religious expression advanced in tandem. If fertile land and military genius were the sources of worldly fortune, the invisible world offered infinite protection if one knew how to speak in the language of the gods.

Gwalior women going to Devipuja

Badoh, Dudahi, Khajuraho, Lokhari, Rikhiyan and Hinglajgadh are testimony to the devotion the kings of Chandella held for the Yoginîs.

Those who desire a deeper understanding of the esoteric traditions of the Chandella should read the two books of Devangana Desai: *The Religious Imagery of Khajuraho,* Project for Indian Cultural Studies, publication IV, Mumbai 1996; and *Erotic Sculpture of India, A Socio-Cultural Study,* Tata McGraw-Hill Publishing Co., New Delhi.

As has been seen, the temples dedicated to the Yoginîs were not part of the orthodox sects.[61] The noble and royal patrons probably followed the esoteric cult without advertising it because, apparently, in following the cult they had to interact with disciples from the lower castes. This might be the reason why no dedicatory stele can be found in any of the temples, making it difficult to attribute their construction to any particular king or queen.

At the beginning of the 10th century the Yoginî temples proliferated throughout the territory of the Chandella. It seems

Khajuraho Traditional
Temple Complex

that the tradition of the Yoginîs there was related to the Mâtrikâs, and as a result a symbolic architecture was developed in the region giving the Yoginî temples a rectangular shape.

Below is a synoptic table of the Yoginî temples in the territory of the Chandella:

Temple	Approximate Date	Shape	Tradition	Number of Yoginîs
Khajuraho	Beginning of the 10th	Rectangular	Mâtrikâs	64+main Devi+2[62]
Rikhijan	Beginning of the 10th	Rectangular	Mâtrikâs	64
Lokhari	Beginning of the 10th	Unknown	Mâtrikâs	Unknown
Dudahi	The 10th century	Circular	Unknown	42
Badoh	The 10th century	Rectangular	Unknown	42
Naresar*	The 10th century	Unknown	Mâtrikâs	Unknown
Miatuli*	The 11th century	Circular	Unknown	64 +main Devi
Hinglajgadh	The 10th century	Unknown	Mâtrikâs	Unknown

---

[61] From various texts we get the impression that the Brahmins priest were even against the cult of the Yoginîs as it represents a threat to their status and power.

[62] Probably Ganga Devi and Jamuna Devi. (Suggested by Dr. Devangana Desai in a private conversation.)

*The temples of Naresar and Mitttauli were built in the territory ruled by the Kachchpaghata, feudal lords of the Chandella during the years 950 to 1050.

5. KHAJURAHO

(Beginning of the 10ᵗʰ Century)

"An Indian myth about creation says that the god Brahma, standing upon an enormous thousand-petaled lotus, turned his eyes simultaneously to the four cardinal points. That four-way point of view, arising from the circle of the lotus, was a type of indispensable preliminary orientation, before he initiated the work of creating the universe."[63]

If up to this point the discussion has focused on the circle of the Yoginîs and the circular temples whose form took inspiration from the centres of energy in the human body (the chakras) or in a magical-religious syncretism, the rectangular temple at Khajuraho opens the door to the concept of an assemblage of Yoginîs in which a hierarchy can be perceived in the sculptures' placement.

Back side of the Khajuraho Yogini Temple

A much larger niche, probably that of the principal Goddess, is found at the opposite extreme from the entrance portal, which is oriented toward the northeast. In Khajuraho is seen for the first time that the first and only rule is to "break all the rules" with respect to the cult of the Yoginîs. In traditional Hindu temples, the idols face toward the four cardinal points (east, south, west,

---

[63] L'Homme et ses symboles, C.G. Jung and Robert Laffont, Paris, 1964, p. 240.

The Yoginî Temples of India

and north). The Yoginî temple in Khajuraho is constructed along a vertical northeast-southwest line (Isâna[64]- Nairitya[65]) and a horizontal southeast- northwest (Agni[66]- Vâyu[67])[68] line.

The rectangular nature of the sanctuary has given rise to much conjecture, with one theory even concluding that it was impossible to construct a circular wall on the angular rock that served as the temple's foundation. This argument is not convincing because it does not address a prehistoric temple but rather one that was built in the 10th century at a time when the skill of the architects had been amply demonstrated throughout all of India. Furthermore, ruins and evidence of other rectangular temples dedicated to the Yoginîs have been discovered near Khajuraho.

The mysterious cult of the Yoginîs adhered to a philosophy that was foreign to logic. If one manages to transcend reason and free oneself of the desire to organize information, it may be possible achieve the first step in absorbing the essence and practices of the Yoginî cult.

The niches of the temple are now empty. The three sculptures that survived the long lapse of time and the destructive work of thieves were transported to the Archaeological Museum and placed in its garden and

[64] Isâna = A form of Shiva that presides over the northeast.
[65] Nairitya = God who presides over fear.
[66] Agni = God of Fire.
[67] Vâyu = God of the winds.
[68] In India there are held to be eight cardinal points which are ruled over by different deities: north, south, east, west, northeast, southeast, southwest, and northwest.

54

warehouse. Special permission from the Archaeological Survey of India in New Delhi is needed to view those stored in the warehouse.

The father of Indian archaeology, Sir Alexander Cunningham, refers in one of his commentaries to a great sculpture of Bhairava-Shiva[69] that was discovered beneath a large pile of stones near the temple. The sculpture, now painted red, was taken to a site near the temple of Varâha which is located in a group of temples to the west of Khajuraho. This Bhairava and the Yoginî, which stood in the principal niche, have in common a floral decoration at the crest of the blocks of stone, a detail that may indicate that the Bhairava formed part of the temple of the Yoginîs.

A sketch drawn in Dr. Vidya Dehejia's book on the Yoginîs shows sixty-five niches, while in her book on Khajuraho Dr. Devangana Desai based her conclusions on an extrapolation from the sizes of the existing niches in the spaces where no feature of the niches remains. The resulting sixty-seven niches correspond with this author's calculations. In addition to the principal niche, the temple apparently housed sixty-six other niches. It is indisputable that the Mâtrikâs were included among the Yoginîs of Khajuraho (the sculptures of Brahmanî and Meheshvarî that Cunningham found in the temple are proof of this).

Mahisamardini
Khajuraho's Hinglaja

The sixty-seven niches indicate that, in addition to the tutelary Goddess, two other Goddesses were added to the sixty-four Yoginîs. It is likely that these were Ganga Devi and Jamuna Devi (associated with the two rivers by those names) because the river goddesses were particularly venerated in northern India. Again it must be understood that

[69] Bhairava-Shiva = The God Shiva, often in his form of Bhairava was the central image in the Yoginî cult.

many questions exist with few answers available. The walls of the Yoginî temple spoke an esoteric and symbolic language that was understood only by the cult's devotees.

Another mystery relates to the question as to why the goddess of the main niche was called Hinghalâja[70], given that she actually Mahishâsuramardinî (the iconography in which she kills the buffalo demon is very well known). At the border between Rajasthan and Madhya Pradesh is a site called Hinglajgadh or Hinglajgarh, Hingalâja's dwelling. At the museum of Indore one can appreciate many sculptures from the Hinglajgadh site and its surroundings, which were rescued when the Gandhi Sagar dam was constructed. The variety of the sculptures demonstrates that Hinglajgadh, from the Buddhist eras of the fourth or fifth centuries, was already an important religious centre. In addition to the deities of the Buddhists, Shakti-worshippers, Jains, Shiva-worshippers and the Vishnu sects, a Mahishâsuramardinî deity with the name Hinglajgadh Devi can be found there. (Just as in the case of Khajuraho). Hinglajgadh and Khajuraho were probably connected through the Hingalâja hill and river in Baluchistan (now in Pakistan) where legend holds that the head of Shiva's consort fell while he wandered in grief carrying her cadaver (other versions speak of her navel). That site, along with other sites where different pieces of the Goddess fell, is sacred to the devotees of the Devi (the Shaktas).

Stories exist which say that Hingalâja was a pilgrimage site for the Nâthas Siddhas, where they carried out initiations into the practices of Yoga. The Nâthas Siddhas, whose teacher was Gorakhnâtha, lived in Khajuraho for a time and perhaps this was the source of the inscription of the name Hinghalâja on the sculpture of the tutelary Devi.

Gorakhnâtha appears in the legends as a disciple of Matsyendranâtha. As previously mentioned, to the latter is attributed the development of the Yoginî cult in addition to his being the author of the *Mahâ-Kaulajñânanirnaya* – an orally

---

[70] Hingula = That which shines like an orange fruit; he whom water cannot wet is waterproof like the lotus flower. It is Lakshmi radiating her beauty.

transmitted doctrine which was subsequently transcribed onto pages made of palm leaves. He was also founder of the Yoginî-Kaula cult and is considered the father of Yoga. The same Guru-disciple legends say that Gorakshanâtha did not hold with the ideas of his Master with regard to the cult of feminity. In many of the tales the disciple Gorakshanâtha tries to "awaken" his master Matsyendranâtha to the mesmerizing charm of female energies.

The Nâtha Siddhas, the Yoginî-Kaula, and many other schools such as that of the Yoga of Patañjali sought then and still seek to attain higher states of consciousness, and thus free themselves from the cycle of birth and death by practicing the Siddhis (extraordinary powers). However, the practitioner runs the risk of finding himself seduced by the display of "supernatural" powers and forgets the ultimate goal of enlightenment. Certain sources indicate that some followers of the Yoginî cult sought a "magic wand" or an ability to instantly conjure up those special powers. It is also probable that the interpretations of such esoteric knowledge were reduced to the level of mere appearance and empty words, without truly exploring a spiritual path. Perhaps this was the process that began the downfall of the Yoginî cult, which attained its height between the ninth and twelfth centuries.

6. DUDHAI (Dudahi)

(10th Century)

The Yoginî sanctuary in Dudhai is located on a small hill. Certain areas of the temple have been destroyed, but it is clear that it was a temple where forty-two divinities were worshipped in their shrine-niches along the circular wall. The entrance is through a portal, which is reached via two lateral stairways. Some stone debris is lying in the middle of the temple where usually altar to Bhairava would be found. Many remains of Dudhai sculptures are now located in the museum at Jhansi.

According to a Muslim historian of the period, towards the end of the first millenium Dudhai was an important center of the Chandellas. Less than a kilometer away from the Yoginîs temple, are found other temples dedicated to Brahma, Vishnu, Shiva and to some Jain saints.

The patron of the temple is thought to be a member of the Chandella dynasty of the 10th century, but as a result of the customary impenetrability of the Yoginî cult, the construction of the Yoginî temple in Dudhai cannot be attributed to any particular king, queen or feudal lord. There was probably some relationship between the Dudhai temple and that of Mitauli given that the columns of the niches in both temples have the same motif, similar also to a number of smaller temples that can be found along one of the ramps leading up to the fortress at Gwalior.

Among the ruins of the traditional temples in Dudhai is an inscription stating that Devalabdhi, grandson of Yasovarman, built the temple dedicated to Brahma.

We noticed that Jain temples are often in the vicinity of the Yoginî temples as it is the case in Dudhai. The Yoginîs are named in Jain texts. In various temples in Rajasthan, the frames and lintels of the doors are adorned with female images that are called "Yoginîs". Representations of Bhairava are also found on the walls adjacent to the altar doors.

The circular temple of Dudhai containing forty-two niches corroborates, the diversity of the tantric cult that worshipped the Yoginîs. Previous mention has been made of the temples of sixty-four and eighty-one Yoginîs. The magic number of sixty-four may have been related to the sixty-four Tantras or with the eight qualities of the eight Mothers. The sacred set of eighty-one Yoginîs may also have had to do with the sacred number nine multiplied by "itself". In Dudhai we now find the unique cult of forty-two goddesses.

The Tantras differ from the distinct spiritual and philosophical currents in India because they were open to a public that sought religious independence regardless of social class, caste or gender. The cult of the Yoginîs was open to women and all who genuinely embarked on the road to spiritual realization. Apparently, the worship of the Yoginîs was flexible and varied in accordance with the material and metaphysical needs of its adherents.

Tantric practices of all kinds are intimately tied to Yoga and the techniques of the Siddhis[71]. The Yoginîs with their specific characteristics might have helped to confront the diverse expressions in which energy expressed itself (anger, jealousy, envy, hate, passion, happiness, etc.). In addressing these emotions (perhaps facing the Yoginî symbolized by that emotion), the adept could begin to free the total energy (Shakti) and let it flow to be absorbed within consciousness. The techniques of the Siddhis help cleanse the system so that the energy moves freely through subtle channels. From the experience of the senses gross levels it is possible to reach the more delicate and sublime levels where "everything" is possible. The siddhis open the awareness to the field of all possibilities and therefore it is important that the adept

---

[71] Siddhis = Esoteric practices within Yoga. While cleaning the system through the practices one achieves "supernatural" powers.

have a high state of consciousness in order not to be tempted to make evil use of his powers. Bhairava is the guardian of the secrets of the Universe and of higher states of consciousness, and probably for that reason his image was the central point in the Yoginî temples.

The number forty-two might be related to an ancient manuscripts[72] in which it is said that to achieve success one should worship the Yoginîs within a magic circle in which forty-two letters of the Sanskrit alphabet were represented. The hierarchic value of the letters of the alphabet are also spoken of in other sacred texts.

Passages are found in the Mahâ-Kaulajñânanirnaya that refer to the sublime value of letters and their sounds. The mantras are the foundation of the meditative experience, and through the states attained by this practice it is possible to begin to enter the knowledge of the siddhis.

"...It is said that the place and inner part of meditation is a clear understanding of Pinda [73]. All proceeds from the letters, and in this is the void state..." (Mahâ-Kaulajñânanirnaya, Patala III, 1-4)

"...Taking each Bija [74] separately from the mass of letters one can achieve any act desired..." (Mahâ-Kaulajñânanirnaya, Patala IV, 16-17)

"...When one meditates that the Devi dwells in our body, stirred by love-bliss, in the right mood for sexual union, she is Sahâja [75]- Shakti [76]. The Kulajâ [77] is the mass of letters, the essence of Kula [78]. What could be unknown by her?" (Mahâ-Kaulajñânanirnaya, Patala VIII, 7-9).

---

[72] Goraksha Samhitâ, which is a simiplified form of the *Srî Matottara Tantra*, see page 31-33

[73] Pinda = Sphere, human body that is transformed, offering to the ancestors.

[74] Bìja = Mystical letter, symbol forming the essence of the mantra of the deity, seed, semen.

[75] Sahâja = Natural state of pure spontaneity; born to be herself.

[76] Shakti = Energy, the creative feminine force, consort of a god.

[77] Kulajâ = Born to be energy

[78] Kula = In some Tantric texts it is synonymous with Shakti (energy). Born of Shakti and Shiva. Family of Brahmans, of the Bengala lineage.

"…Fix one's attention on the forehead with the mass of letters. (Then) in many ways one becomes eloquent, experiencing trembling of the limbs[79]. Nâda [80] exhales forth and one feels a great breeze. Through continued application one may take whatever shape one desires." (Mahâ-Kaulajñânanirnaya, Patala XIV, 69-70).

"… Meditate on the centre of the mass of letters in the space between the eyebrows. Constant practice of this worship one may become an eternal hero, able to reject ordinary rules. O You, loved by Yoginîs, one becomes like the cause of both creation and dissolution, always free of fever and death. There is no doubt about it. Applying this method of knowledge, one becomes liberated." (Mahâ-Kaulajñânanirnaya, Patala XIV, 71-73)

The knowledge and practices preserved in the Mahâ-Kaulajñânanirnaya manuscript should not be taken literally because it deliberately employed an abstruse language. The preceding verses permit an exploration of the symbolism of the force of the letters and, therefore, the mantras which form an essential part of Yoga and the practices associated with the Yoginîs. The word Yoginî was originally the feminine counterpart of the word Yogî. When the Yoginîs of the temples are mentioned, the reference is not to women of flesh and blood. Nevertheless, the energy that exists in the Yoginî-woman who has attained higher states of consciousness is essentially the same divine energy represented by the sculptures of the Yoginîs in the temples.

Dudhai was probably a temple where the practices were more oriented to the secret sounds of mantras than to other limbs of Yoga or Tantra where more space would have been required.

Dudhai Forty-two Yogini Temple

---

[79] The yogi practicing the siddhis experience «trembling of the limbs » before levitation

[80] Nâda = Strong nasal sound, mantra

7. BADOH

(10ᵗʰ Century)

The temple known as Gadarmal lies eighteen kilometers from the village of Kulhar. A peasant recounted to this author the legend of a shepherd who lost his flock during the night. Without time for rest or food, the next day the man wandered through the fields seeking his flock and when night came he slept exhausted in the fields. That night he dreamed that his sheep had risen to the Infinite to seek the Mothers of the Universe and, having found them, took refuge in their arms. Each Goddess sang a particular sound. As a result of the vibration coming from those harmonious sounds, the sheep multiplied. On awakening, the shepherd saw his sheep grazing at the edge of a nearby pond. From that moment, he never lacked for money and his business was blessed with abundance. In gratitude, he decided to build a temple to the Mothers.

Many theories exist about the form of the original sanctuary. One theory refers to a rectangular temple in which forty-two small niches fit around the platform that today serves as a base for the temple to "the Mothers" of Gardarmal, which was constructed with shaped stones apparently taken from nearby ruins. This current temple is of traditional form with a portico in front.

Gardamal Temple

One of the criteria for selecting sites for temples to the Yoginîs appears to have been the presence of a rocky height near a pond or river, similar to the topography of the Badoh site. On the slope of one of the nearby hills are caves where saints of different faiths probably lived. Fruit trees grace the fields and shepherds can still be seen resting in lofty homes where they watch over their sheep, as if no time had passed since the ancient days.

Eighteen fragments from the sculptures of a variety of Goddesses were discovered in Badoh.

Ultimately, the construction of the current temple must have something to do with the legend of the shepherd, while the temple to the Yoginîs was probably built years earlier by an unknown king of the Chandella dynasty. The area where the Badoh and Dudahi temples were built was under the control of the Chandella kings some of whom, as has been noted, were devotees of the Yoginîs.

It is said that the Yoginîs flew through the air in groups taking on the appearance of insects, birds or women of flesh and blood, who when they landed sang and danced in a circle as if they were a vibrating chakra of energy.

The cardinal points are fixed in the geometry of the temple's circle, and out of these arise the angular forms. The Chandella kings constructed a number of Yoginî temples of rectangular shape – that of Badoh apparently belongs to this tradition.

Instead of worshipping sixty-four Yoginîs, the temples of Badoh and Dudahi venerated forty-two Goddesses. This magic number corresponds to the group of letters of the Sanskrit alphabet[81] known as Bhûtapali in which forty-two letters are identified as special divine beings.

Feminie sculpture from Badoh site

---

[81] The Sanskrit alphabet contains 42 letters (varNas): 9 vowels (svaras) and 33 consonants (vyanjanas). Sanskrit has 48 phonemes (Vedic Sanskrit has 49).

The Yoginîs were invoked as protectors of the kings and their lands, their subjects and beasts, and everything that surrounded them, as well as to guard the territory against calamities caused by wars, invasions, epidemics and other adversities.

The Masters of the Tantric tradition of the Yoginî cult most certainly interpreted esoteric knowledge and applied to the construction of the temples the criteria of auspicious numbers and geometric forms which fostered the fulfillment of the desires and ambitions of their patrons. The mystery of the Yoginî temples remains as impenetrable as an unread book.

8. MITAULI (Mitâvali)

(11ᵗʰ Century?)

The road to Mitauli from Gwalior passes near Padhauli where the restoration work on the principal temple is being carried out. Bit by bit the scattered stones begin to regain their former dignity. Like a mirage between planted fields, a rocky hill crowned with the stone temple of Mitauli rises near a pond graced with blossoming lotus flowers. As with all the temples dedicated to the Yoginîs, a palpable silence fills the air above the ageless rock. Mute and empty, the sixty-five niches give rise to images visible only in the imagination, and a new series of questions arise.

Due to the decorations on the frame and the base, the sixty-fifth niche can probably be attributed to the great Devi. As in Ranipur Jharial and Hirapur, the altar to Shiva-Bhairava is located in the center.

The stonewall of the temple speaks of solidity and immovability while its circular form simultaneously suggests movement. Within the open-air temple of Mitauli, the stone floor is flat; however, a progressive and nearly imperceptible incline directs any rain that might fall on it towards the single discreet drain.

No sculpture of the Yoginîs remains in the niches. Doctor Deheija states in her work on the Yoginîs that a sculpture now located at the Fowler Museum in Los Angeles possibly comes from the Mitauli temple. Her reasoning is based on the similar iconography of one of the sculptures from the Naresar[82] workshop now located in the San Antonio Museum of Art in USA. The

---

[82] The Naresar and Mitauli sites were situated in the territory of the Chandella feudal lords.

image and attributes of the two sculptures are similar. Both Yoginîs are seated on an owl. Both are fearful images, of those Yoginîs who lurk at night eager to devour flesh or corpses. Only the execution of the work varies between the two sculptures. The Yoginî of Naresar is an example of the simplest form of Yoginî, while that which ostensibly comes from Mitauli is far more elaborate. The Naresar temple probably dates from the early part of the 11th century, and the Mitauli from its final

years. The temples are located relatively near one another.

As with the other Yoginî temples, dates give rise to controversy. Various inscriptions are found at Mitauli that were written at different times and for different sovereigns. One which has deteriorated refers to a date that corresponds to the year 1323 of the western calendar and mentions a king Maharaja Devapala and his queen. Did they sponsor the construction

Central Shrine

of the temple? Or were they patrons who were responsible for its restoration, when decorations were added to the outside walls?

The contents of the niches were replaced by simple lingas without bases. Generally, in temples where lingas are worshipped as a symbol of Shiva, the phallus rests on a base shaped like a Yoni (the vulva of the Goddess). It appears that over the centuries some unknown patron wanted to make the temple more masculine. The Shakti-worshippers (those who worshipped the female divine energy) and the Tantric sects (including the Yoginî cult and its temples) were not always favorably received by the orthodox worshippers from the traditional sects[83].

The *Mahâ-Kaulajñânanirnaya* states that a material linga (e.g. of stone or metal) should not be worshipped, and that one should only worship a linga mentally. Whoever placed the lingas in the niches of the Mitauli temple was either unaware of the cult of the Yoginîs or wanted it forgotten.

*Worshipping this body **linga**, one may obtain both liberation and enjoyment. **Devi**, it is the **linga** giving **Siddhi**, stationed in the body, steady and strong. Whosoever should always meditate on this mental **linga**, for such a one is*

---

[83] Two principal currents exist in Hinduism: worshippers of Shiva and those who worship Vishnu.

achieved the pre-eminent and highest self-knowledge. Mahâ-Kaulajñânanirnaya, Patala III, 27-28)

*Thus, **O Devi**, have been declared the characteristics of the **Kaulika** body **linga**. Any other (**linga**) one should abandon, such as those made of stone, wood or clay. The ordinary path is devoid of success and liberation. (Mahâ-Kaulajñânanirnaya, Patala III, 29-30).*

The Mitauli temple is well preserved and provides visitors an opportunity to imagine for themselves the sixty-four Yoginîs with their tutelary Devi and Bhairava. The serene atmosphere of the round, open air temple invites one to sit and meditate. Transcending rational thought, time or physical barriers, the Yoginîs perhaps may come to dance within the Divine....

9. NARESAR

(10th Century to Early 11th Century)

As previously demonstrated, only three temples with their Yoginîs survived both invasions and the lapse of time, and although the former furnished new ideologies they also produced the vandalism that stemmed from ignorance and lack of respect for the doctrines that existed in the lands that were conquered. Ranipur Jharial, Hirapur and Bheragat provide valuable information on the Yoginî cult that extended throughout a vast territory and which remained active for more than four centuries.

Naresar Yogini illustration

There also exists the mute testimony of temples that are empty or in ruins (Mitauli, Khajuraho, Dudahi, Badoh,[84] MauSuhania[85]) as well as various groups of sculptures found in places where practically no feature of the temple remains and where the Yoginîs were worshipped. (Naresar, Shadol, Lokhari, Rikhiyan, Hinglajgadh, Kanchipuram). Nevertheless, in places where at one time there existed an open-sky

---

[84] In Badoh, the Gadarmal temple took posession of the platform.

[85] Devangana Desai, The religious Imagery of Khajuraho, photos 88 and 89.

temple (either circular or rectangular) although no trace of such can now be found, it would appear that the spell of divine energies yet circulates among the errant molecules of the air. This is the case of Naresar.

A solitary road ends at the site of a few temporary shelters near the base of a rocky hill. The people of the neighboring villages fear to enter upon the road to Naresar and attribute their reluctance to the possible presence of guerrillas (Naxalites) who might seek refuge in uninhabited areas.

At the time the temples were constructed, their devout worshippers sought isolated places of wind-stripped rock in order to perform their rites, almost as if they needed the freedom of the air that circulated between the statues of the Yoginîs in order to understand the impenetrable doctrines and decipher messages hidden in symbols. Even today the temples are found in remote locations, distant from urban noise and pollution.

Attracted by the energy and power that was felt, and is yet felt at the Naresar site, other sects also constructed their temples there. A number of temples dedicated to Shiva survive in Naresar. One of these – although much smaller – is similar to that of Teli-ka Mandir found in the fortress of Gwalior. They are the only two temples in all of India where the architecture of the north is intermingled with the rules of south Indian architecture. A short distance beyond this group of temples, a rocky hill is reflected in a pond. One's imagination can easily begin to outline on the empty rock an austere stone temple where the Yoginîs of Naresar resided.

At the beginning of the 20th century, twenty sculptures of the Yoginîs were transported from Naresar to the Archaeological Museum of Gwalior, which is located within one of the entrances to the fortress city. The Yoginîs have inscriptions which state their names and even give them numbers, but the calligraphy is not carefully executed as if it was the work of a scribe of lesser talent. It is hard to imagine that the workshop where the beautiful and detailed sculptures of Naresar were created had contracted a mere apprentice to carve the names of the Yoginîs on their pedestals.

The Yoginî named Vihâra has an inscribed date of "Samvat 1245" which corresponds to the year 1189 of our era. Nevertheless, the style of the Naresar Yoginîs is typical of the tenth century, not as well worked as the style of the twelfth. To put a date on the sculptures, the historian Vidya Dehejia relied on the style and not on the inscriptions which – according to her – could have been done at a later date, when the temple was renovated, for example.

Yogini illustration from Naresar workshop
The original is at San Antonio Museum of Art, USA

10. LOKHARI

(Beginning of the 10th Century)

"Each (divine archetype), in particular, responds to the differences of disposition, inclination, idiosyncrasy and intellectual acumen of the people; accordingly each person should focus on his own spiritual goal and enter upon the path that leads to it."[86]*...Ramón N. Prats*

The statutes of the Lokhari Yoginîs are fascinating not for their refined style or the quality of the workmanship but for the theme in which heads of beasts appear on the bodies of voluptuous women. Each Yoginî appears to arise out of great blocks of stone more than a meter and a half in height. Some have a tiny image engraved on its pedestal which represents an animal, its corresponding Varaha (vehicle).

Yogini from Lokhari

When Dr. Dehejia visited the Lokhari site in the 1980s, she found twenty figures of Yoginîs reclining among scattered stones that probably belonged to the temple. When

---

[86] El Libro Tibetano de los Muertos (The Tibetan Book of the Dead), edition of Ramón N. Prats, in a discourse explaining the divinities and divine archetypes of tantric hermeneutics.

visiting the site more than twenty years later, this author found only a few pieces of the figures remaining. It seems that the constant theft of the sculptures mentioned by Dr. Dehejia in her book worsened over the years. Left unprotected at the isolated site of Lokhari, the Yoginî statues became easy prey for unscrupulous dealers who designed ways for making them disappear.

In the town of Rypura is a Yoginî that has been rescued from the hands of such criminals and transformed into the tutelary goddess for the local police station. She is the Yoginî with the face of a bear. The Yoginî with the face of a snake had no such luck. Only a portion of her head can be found in the fortress at Garwha en route to Allahabad. Between the walls of the fortress are a number of temples. To one side, in a storage area protected by a fence, pieces of sculptures can be found that were recovered from the surrounding region. It is difficult to find someone to open the storage area but it is possible to identify from the

Snake headed Yogini

fence the Yoginîs of Rikhiyan and the portion of the sculpture of the Yoginî with the head of a snake. Perhaps other Yoginîs are hidden away in the area and will soon be displayed in the museum that is being constructed within the fortress.

According to Dr. Dehejia, only three of the twenty sculptures that she found at Lokhari had human faces, and those three were Mâtrikâs. (Aindirî's head bore a crown, a thunderbolt in one hand and was being carried by an elephant; Vaishnavî, also crowned, had four arms and Garuda[87] at her feet; and Châmunda, with her

---

[87] Garuda = The eagle, the vehicle that carries Vishnu and therefore also Vaisnavi.

garland of skulls, was seated resting her two feet on a man and in her four arms carried the emblems of Shiva while devouring a chunk of flesh out of a skull-cup.)

The Lokhari site is situated in a remote locale far from any urban environment, much like the other places that were chosen ages ago for the construction of temples to the Yoginîs.

The mystery of the beast heads as it pertains to the Yoginîs is revealed here as a fundamental theme. In some sects Shiva appears as the Lord of animals, Pasupathi. It is said that the Pasupatha sect was founded or reformed by Lakulisa, a saint who popularized the cult of Shiva during the time when Buddhism was at its height. Pasu means animal or bonds, and Pathi means God. Apparently, through adoration and devotion to Lord Shiva one may transcend the bonds through which a person becomes imprisoned by the senses (as animals).

One of the many legends about the Lord of animals tells that Shiva became bored with being constantly worshipped in Kashi (Varanasi) and transformed himself into a gazelle in order to live freely among the other animals in the forest. Brahma, Vishnu and the other gods were unable to tolerate Shiva living exiled from Kashi and went in search of him. On capturing the gazelle, they broke one of its horns. Vishnu took the horn to Nepal where even today it is worshipped in Pashupatinath (the temple in Deopatan on the outskirts of Katmandu) as a linga (phallus). Since that time Shiva was declared to be the Lord of the beasts.

Shiva-Pasupathi took on great significance during the expansion of Tantra. The Buddhists of Nepal associated Pasupathi with Avalokiteswara just as they associated Matsyendranâtha (the founder of the Yoginî cult) with him. Pasupathi is also worshipped as a protector of the Sakya Buddhist schools in Tibet and is represented on the rear walls of their Gompas[88] in nude form accompanied by his Devi, with an erect phallus like Yogeshvara, Lord of Yoga.

---

[88] Gompa = Buddhist temple, called Vihara in Sanskrit, often adjoining monasteries.

As one might suppose, the various religious currents became mixed and were adapted to a number of popular beliefs. The

school that worshipped the beast-headed Yoginîs in Lokhari probably had rituals and Yoga practices in which they sought to free themselves from the bonds associated with one animal or another. Here again, only the austere and silent walls of stone witnessed the practices and rituals of the Yoginî cult.

Lokhari Yogini at Rypura police station

11. RIKHIYAN

(Beginning of the 10th Century)

Rikhiyan lies near Lokhari, close to the south shore of the Jamuna River in an agricultural area. The site consists of a few caves containing a bubbling spring. A number of temple ruins are indeed there but no trace remains of the temple dedicated to the Yoginîs.

Set of four Yoginis from Rikhiyan
Original at Gadhwa fortress near Allahabad

The Yoginîs of Rikhiyan are seated in a posture known as the Lalita asana. Currently, none of the Yoginîs are found at their original site. Three blocks were transported to the fortress at Gadhwa, fifty kilometers from Allahabad[90]. The sculptures are stored there in a warehouse protected by a locked fence. Another stone block is preserved in the Denver Museum in the United States. Among the Yoginîs discovered in Rikhiyan are the Mâtrikâs Chamunda

---

[90] They are stored at the same place like the remains of the Lokhari's Yoginîs.

and Varahî. Because the stone blocks consist of four sculptures each, it is possible to speculate with some degree of certainty that the temple must have been dedicated to a group of sixty-four Yoginîs (a multiple of four). The lengthwise of the stones where the sets of four Yoginîs were carved indicates that the temple must have been rectangular.

No flat space can be seen near the Rikhiyan caves which may have held the temple, but at a nearby site on the shore of a pond it is possible to visualize the walls of the temple containing the sixty-four Yoginîs of Rikhiyan.

Among the discovered Rikhiyan sculptures can be found one Yoginî with the head of a horse riding an animal that is half-chameleon and half wild boar. It bears a maul, a type of bell, something appearing to be a corpse, and a decapitated head. The next Yoginî also bears a maul, a sword, a bowl-like half of a skull, and a corpse. Logically, this style of image leads to the belief that the rites carried out in the temple were bloody in nature. But as previously mentioned, in the Tantras and probably also in the Yoginî cult – as indicated in the *Mâha-Kauljñanairnaya* – the rites were based on metaphysical ideas expressed through a code. The paragraph quoted below from the *Mâha-Kauljñanairnaya* speaks of the symbolic nature of the offerings used in the rites.

*Devi, a **Kaulika**[91] should worship this to attain the desired **Siddhi**[92], mentally using flowers, sweets, essence of incense, etc. (Mâha-Kauljñanairnaya, Patala III, 24).*

The first flower represents doing no harm, the second is self-control, the third is generosity, the fourth the correct temperament, the fifth is compassion and the sixth is the divestment of all cruelty. The seventh flower is meditation and the eighth is knowledge. Discerning these laws, in relation

[91] Kaulika = Adepts of Kaula, specialists in Kundalini Yoga, disciples of Kulâchârya, a Master. He who knows that liberation comes from Kula. Belonging to the school of the Kaulas which is closely related to the cult of the Yoginîs.

[92] Siddhi = Attainment of superhuman or magic powers, Enlightenment.

*to the flowers, one should worship this mental **Linga**. (Mâha-Kauljñanairnaya, Patala III, 25-26).*

Vessels are mentioned elsewhere and the best of these is said to be the cranium of a wise man to whom the hymns of the Rig Veda are attributed. The Vedas represent the essence of the traditional knowledge.

***Bhairava** said, "Devi! Listen carefully concerning the nature of the vessels. A vessel of **Kaulika** may be made of clay, tortoise shell, the metal of bells, copper, iron, gold, silver, mother of pearl, conch, horn, wood or stone.*

*Best of all is the cranium of **Vishvâmitra** [93]. If one drinks, enjoys and eats from it, one is the Lord, beyond the Lord, and even greater than this. One should only drink wine from this wide vessel that is like the shell of a coconut. **Devi**, the types of vessels and the manner of action have been told. What more do you wish to know? (Mâha-Kauljñanairnaya, Patala VII, 11-16).*

***Devi** said, "Lord of sounds! Thanks to You I have attained the divine state. Lord God! By Your grace I have come to understand the qualities of knowledge. (Mâha-Kauljñanairnaya, Patala VII, 17).*

The following paragraph speaks of going beyond appearances by not limiting the mind to the mere meaning of words and concepts. The goal of Yoga is the state of unity where no differences exist. The energy of the Universe, though expressed in a variety of ways, is "in essence" one alone.

*One should perceive foul odors or beautiful fragrances as equal. **Suresvari** [94], just as the lotus blossom whose petals remain without blemish in the water, so the **Yogi** remains unperturbed when faced with either merit or sin. Wherever this mental state is found, there exists no difference between*

---

[93] Vishvâmitra = One of the seven sages to whom various hymns of the Rig Veda are attributed.

[94] Suresvari = One of the names that Bhairava gives to the Devi in the *Mahâ-Kauljñanairnaya.*

Brahmanism or the **Asvamedha** [95] sacrifice, there will be no difference whether one bathes in the **tîrthas** [96] or has contact with **mlecchas** [97]. (*Mahâ-Kauljñanairnaya, Patala XI, 27-29*).

As can be seen in the preceding paragraphs, as well as in many Buddhist and Tantric texts, imparted knowledge is expressed metaphorically in the dialogue between the God and His Devi. Often the teachings were transcribed during periods in which the authors sought to protect the knowledge through symbols, so that those who were not true devotees or who lacked the guidance of a master would be lost in the words and perhaps become frightened upon imagining the unfolding of strange practices and magic spells.

Animal headed Yogini

The Tantras speak of offerings called the five M's, and some devotees offer the following to the deities: wine (Madya), meat (Mamsa), fish (Matsya), grains (Mudrâ)[98] and coitus (Maithuna).

In the *Kularnava Tantra* it is said that wine (Madya) is not liquor but rather energy which leads the practitioner to the state of *Brahman*[99]. Just as liquor provides a certain state of euphoria, the "wine-energy" is the awakening of the energy of the chakras[100] that vitalizes and provides the "great" bliss.

---

[95] Asvamedha = Bloody sacrifice of any kind of animal.

[96] Tirtha = Place of pilgrimage, sacred place for ritual baths; teacher.

[97] Mlecchas = Foreigner, a person ignorant of the sacred texts, sinner.

[98] Mudrâ = It also means hand or body postures that should increase the flow of energy in the body and mind

[99] Where man attains the true divine image.

[100] Chakras = Centers of energy in the body.

Mamsa: Meat is one of the seven elements of the body: rakta (blood); rasa (moist essence); majja (veins); ashti (bones) sukra (semen); meda (marrow) and mamsa (meat). The Tantra says that the man in the state of ignorance is like a pasu (animal). In symbolic terms, sacrificing an animal is like "killing" ignorance in order to elevate oneself to the level of knowledge.

Matsya: Fish, which in the great majority of cultures is the symbol of the element in which it moves, swimming through the depths and creating turbulence in its own element[101]. In some Tantric texts, the fish is synonymous with the mind when it swims in the ocean of the senses; it symbolizes that which unsettles the mind. Offering the fish would be symbolic of removing all that which prevents the mind from being clear and thus to re establish the proper perception by the senses.

Mudrâ: Grains. This would be whole or cooked rice which is offered in the rites. Food nourishes the body and gives it energy. Mudrâ also signifies a symbolic posture to transmit energy to different parts of the body. Some Tantras speak of eight kinds of mudrâs that have to do with the feelings of desire, greed, anger, lust, envy, etc.

Maithuna: Coitus. The union of man and woman. Complementary opposites. It is the union of the energy of Shakti and Shiva. It is the energy that rises through the energy centers of the spine to arrive at the head in order to achieve transformation, alchemy.

These interpretations do not correspond with some commentaries on the Tantric texts. Often, when one text refers to animal sacrifices and to offerings of blood or semen, it is believed that this was the case in certain rites. Thus, when the Yoginî appears in its iconography to be eating meat, holding a cranium-cup in the hand or standing on a corpse, etc., she is thought to be a dark deity whose appetites must be satiated with bloody offerings. Rarely does the common literature of the people refer to a purely symbolic interpretation, as in the case of the mystical Tantric texts in which knowledge was transmitted through allegories.

[101] The fish swims in the deepest parts of the oceans, rivers, and lakes, etc., stirring up the soil from the bottom and muddying the water.

12. VARANASI

The Yoginîs are bound to Varanasi by the current of popular stories and pious books that speak of the city. A legend tells that in the time when Shiva decided to establish himself in Kashi[102], he had to invoke the circle of powerful Yoginîs so that they could fool Divodâsa – the evil king of Kashi – with their powers and thus expel him from that sacred place. The Yoginîs answered the call. They went out from their abodes of insect-infected brushwood on Mandara Mountain[103] and from every hiding place that sheltered them. Flying faster than the wind they reached Varanasi. Altering their appearance, they took up the activities of astrologers, ascetics, merchants, gardeners, servants, and dancers. They infiltrated the people and with their powers of persuasion convinced them to rise up against the king and frightened him in innumerable other ways. When the king fled, terrified, they were so happy with their new bodies, with bathing in the sacred waters of the Ganges and enjoying the wonders of the place, that they did not wish leave Kashi even though they had achieved their task.

Chousatti Ghat

It is also said that in Varanasi a temple existed that was dedicated to the sixty-four Yoginîs. But today

---

[102] Kashi is one of the names of Varanasi.

[103] Mandara Mountain = Mythical mountain, axis or basis of the tension between the Devas (gods) and Demons in the myth of the process of the creation of the universe.

all that remains is the name of Chousatti Ghat[104] and the temple of Chousatti Devi[105], which is dedicated to the Devi and is located amongst the narrow and dirty streets of Varanasi. For those who wish to visit, the best method is to travel up the river in a small boat from the Chousatti Ghat. The traffic, noise and chaos of the city disappear when riding up the waters of the sacred river and, as if in another dimension, chants and religious rites fill the air. Also, when one wishes to experience the old city, the best way is to walk up the sacred stairs (Ghats) – if the level of the river allows it – or travel in a small boat from one place to another to access the narrow streets and picturesque cubbyholes. The other method for exploring the city is to take a rickshaw[106]. Many residents of Varanasi transport themselves on motorbikes.

The city has grown in layers along the right shore of the river. Varanasi does not leave the visitor in an indifferent mood. It is a city where extreme piety and the most trivial acts of daily life constantly blend together. The city is

Ganga Mahal Ghat

mysterious and difficult to comprehend; one constantly leaps from moments of communion and respect with the piety of its saints and devotees, to displeasure with the pervasive and shameless huckstering of religion.

To a pious native, visiting Varanasi (and dying there in particular) is a way of freeing oneself from reincarnation, the cycle of birth and death. Millions of pilgrims, believing they have reached the

---

[104] Ghat (stairs), sixty-four in number.
[105] Sixty-four Goddesses.
[106] Motorcycles and bicycles with chairs for passengers.

end of their lives, seek refuge there and join the city's many *sannyasis*[107] and beggars.

Throughout the centuries, many philosophers, thinkers and religious men and women have found inspiration in Varanasi. To visit specialized libraries like the Pilgrim Book House (near Durgakund Road) and Harmony Bookshop – both in the Godaulia area – is like exploring a cave filled with wonders. Varanasi invites reading. The mind eagerly seeks out words and ideas to make sense of the experiences lived every day by its inhabitants; to try to understand the past, present, and future of the city that was destroyed repeatedly but somehow manages to keep lively its many resurrections along with the mystery of immortality.

According to the legend, when the Yoginîs assumed human form they became mesmerized with the city and did not want to leave it. Perhaps, among the alleys of Varanasi or along the river the Yoginîs still come and go; or maybe they have flown to a lonely place to unfold the silence that was hidden within the hubbub of the city.

---

[107] People who have renounced family or work to follow a spiritual path.

13. HINGLAJGARH

(10th Century)

The name of the Hinglajgarh site means "the residence of Hinglaj". In fact, a fortress did exist there that apparently protected the goddess Hinglaj. The goddess' name refers to a rock hill in Baluchistan, Pakistan, on the shore of the Aghora River that some call the Hingal or the Hingula. Legend has it that when Shiva wandered disconsolately with the corpse of his consort Sati on his shoulders, her head fell there (other legends say it was her navel). When it (navel or head) fell to the earth, it became transformed into the sacred stone known as Mata, Maha, Maya, Hingula or Hinglaj Devi. As in the other sacred places where parts of the Devi fell, the divinity is represented by a stone. The muslims also worship the goddess Hinglaj, and they call her Bibi Nani or simply Nani, which may be a syncretism of the ancient semitic goddess Anhita.

Hingula means "cinnabar". Cinnabar is natural mercuric sulfide, bright red in color and out of which mercury is extracted. This element is used in traditional Indian medicine, particularly against snakebites and to eliminate poisons and is therefore associated with the cure of all types of illnesses. As it has been mentioned before, out of cinnabar is distilled mercury, which in turn is a universal

Mahisamardinî

alchemical symbol, the passive moist principle, femininity. The relationship between mercury and sulfur (which is found in cinnabar) is the basis of the union of the feminine and masculine principles.

All of these details make it understandable why the Hinglaj site was a place of peregrination. A circular pond of great depth is found between a mountain chain one day's travel from the coast. Some say that some pilgrims submerge themselves in the pond and through an underground passage arrive purified at another part of the mountain. Another rite exists in which coconuts are thrown

Chamunda

with great force into the pond and the amount of bubbles that surface determines the intensity of the pilgrim's happiness.

The Hinglajgadh site in Madya Pradesh was probably consecrated and denominated using the name of the Hinglaj Devi of Pakistan, inasmuch as certain symbols once corresponded to the two places. More than five hundred sculptures were discovered around Hinglajgadh, among them many fragments of Yogin sculptures and sufficient quantity to deduce that a temple dedicated to the Yogins existed there.

The Yogin sculptures are beautiful and finely chiseled in the style pertaining to the second half of the tenth century. There are various Mâtrikâs among the group of Yogins, which confirms that the Yogins of Hinglajgadh belonged to the tradition of Yogins which held that they were born out of the multiplication of the Mâtrikâs.

Many fragments of Yogin"s can be found in the state museum of Bhopal, and four Yogin"s in good condition are displayed in the Birla Museum of Bhopal - Chamunda, Maheshwari Trimurti, Indranî, and Mahishâsuramardinî.

In a previous chapter we discussed about various historians that have found strange that in Khajuraho, one can read "Hinghalâja" on the pedestal of the goddess Mahishâsuramardinî in her well-known iconography in which she kills the buffalo demon Mahishâ. Also, in the museum of Indore there can be found in addition to deities of the Shaktas, Jain, Shaivas, and Vaishna sects out of Hinglajgadh, a deity of Mahishâsuramardinî bearing the name "Hinglajgadh Devi" who probably was the tutelary goddess of that site and who perhaps presided over the group of Yoginîs. (As it was apparently the case in Khajuraho). The patronage of the Yoginî temple at Hinglajgadh is attributed to the Chandella dynasty, which also would have constructed the important religious centre of Khajuraho.

Currently at the Hinglajgadh site are only found the ruins of what was a fort near a great pond in the middle of an uninhabited area. As in every site where temples to the Yoginîs were constructed, there prevails the subtle energy of the magic junction points where portals were opened to communicate with heaven or the underworld…

14. KANCHIPURAM

The sculptures originating from the only group of Yoginîs found to date in southern India are the cause of endless speculation. At the beginning of the 20th century, the well-known specialist and collector of Indian art Jouveau-Debreuil recovered a dozen sculptures which became known as the Yoginîs of Kanchipuram. It is not clear whether Jouveau-Debreuil found these sculptures in the town of Kanchipuram or somewhere in that district. These sculptures of the goddesses are of great size and must have been housed in a building of large dimension. There are many possible

Kanchipuram Yogini, original at the Musée Guimet, Paris

locations around Kanchipuram that could have been the site of the temple, such as on the shore of lotus-covered ponds where lonely rock-strewn hills rise and where stone stairways can still be seen. Tamil Nadu is a region rich in granite and marble which lends itself to the construction of large sculptures. Artists can be seen shaping these stones along the roadways.

In the Archaeological Museum of Chennai there is a severely-damaged sculpture of a Yoginî (headless and missing three of its arms), along with other sculptures in a similar style and which originate in regions where the Chola dynasties reigned during the 10th century.

Doctor Dehejia speculates that a king of the Kaveripakkan region (northeast of Kanchipuram) constructed the temple for his protection, copying the invading monarchs who brought with them from the north the concept of the Yoginîs as bestowers of power and strength. It appears that some few sculptures were found in Kaveripakkan of a style similar to that of the Yoginîs.

The Kanchipuram Yoginîs have given rise to other theories. One of these states that the Yoginîs may have belonged to a temple dedicated solely to the Mâtrikâs, as was the custom in Orissa. This theory has some substance because among the sculptures collected by Joueau-Debreuil is a statue of Shiva appa rently playing a Vina (a stringed instrument)[108]. In the Sathalapura sanctuary in Orissa is a series of Mâtrikâs from the 10th century, each

Kanchipuram Yogini, original at the Musée Guimet, Paris

carved out of a stone block and seated in the position of lalita asana, accompanied by a Shiva playing the Vina. But the group of goddesses from Kanchipuram is not of the iconography depicting peaceful mothers accompanied by infants – such as was the custom in Orissa of depicting the Mâtrikâs during that period. On the contrary, the Yoginîs of Kanchipuram bear aggressive symbols and their entire aspect is violent in nature.

Because the goddesses found in Kanchipuram were only eleven in number, attempts have been made to corroborate the theory that the southern temple was not of the Yoginîs. Some researchers have based their theory on the fact that a tradition

[108] This sculpture is located in the Museum of Fine Arts in Boston.

Kanchipuram Yogini, original at
the Musée Guimet, Paris

also existed of worshipping sixteen Mothers, and have attempted to apply the name of Mâtrikâs to the Yoginîs. But the goddess designed as Châmundâ -because of her drooping breasts-has an iguana as a steed, and this has nothing in common with Châmundâ iconography. The other two of this set of three displayed at the Musée Guimet also have disorderly tresses like Châmundâ, and they all display certain ferocity with fangs extruding from the edges of wide-open mouths.

The Yoginîs of Kanchipuram are notable for their sensuality. Their lips are fleshy and their bodies and gestures flow with feminine grace and voluptuousness.

It is worthwhile visiting the Archaeological Museum of Chennai to compare the styles. In Europe the Yoginîs of Kanchipuram are located in the Guimet museum of Paris, in the British Museum in London, and in the Reitberg Museum of Zurich. In North America, the Yoginîs visited the Royal Ontario Museum of Toronto and museums in Washington, D.C., Minneapolis, Detroit and Kansas City.

Kanchipuram Yogini, original at
the Sackler Gallery of Arts,
Washington D.C.

15. DELHI- YOGINÎPURA

The various Devi cults along with the Tantric and Shakti-worshipper sects also developed in great measure in the northern and eastern regions of the Indian subcontinent. These probably influenced the Yoginî cults in the central and northeastern zones where ruins of Yoginî temples are also found. Although no temples or Yoginî sculptures survived in western India, it is said that three temples existed in Gujarat: one in the village of Kamli in the Sidhpur district, and the other in the village of Palodhar in the Mehsana district. But the most interesting reference is found in certain ancient Jain[109] texts which stated that important Yoginî temples existed in Broach in the state of Gujarat, in Ajmer in Rajasthan, in Ujjain in western Madhya Pradesh and in Yoginîpura in the current state of Delhi.

Sanskrit Kendra and Museums, New Delhi

Historically, eight cities continually flourished on the plains near the Jamuna River where the city of Delhi is now located. The first four developed around the *Qutb Minar*[110] minaret. One of the first names given to the city was *Indraprastha*, which is mentioned in the great epic poem, the *Mahabharata*; and as previously stated

---

[109] The Jain religion is one of the oldest spiritual doctrines of India.
[110] Dr. Supla Kumar said in his book about Delhi that a great millstone that became later on the Qtub Minar was in place before the Muslim invasions.

Delhi was spoken of as *Yoginîpura* in the ancient Jain literature. From the 12th century forward other cities arose as a result of the Muslim dynasties, and today Delhi flourishes with many interesting sites that are testimony to its Muslim past. A large selection of literature and guidebooks exists concerning these and other sites. With regard to the Yoginîs, this author recommends the book <u>*Delhi, City of Yoginis*</u> by Supla Kumar, who dedicates his work to *Yogamaya* whose temple is located in Mehrauli, a short

Sanskrit Kendra and Museums, New Delhi

distance from Qtub Minar. Also worthwhile is a tour through the Archaeological Park of Mehrauli. And following the Mehrauli Gurgaon roadway, one passes Sanskriti Kendra with its Museum of Terracota where one can see common items of daily usage that are extraordinary treasures, in addition to the location being a veritable refuge of peace. The same road leads to Gurgaon where the American Institute of Indian Studies can be found in the institutional area of that satellite city, and whose library is one of the best and most complete of India. Substantial information about the Yoginî cult can be accessed there.

91

16. GUWAHATI

According to various legends Master Matsyendranâth experienced the revelation of the Yoginî cult in the country of Kâmarûpa[111]. This probably referred to the territory between Nilachal Hill – where the goddess Kâmâksa[112] resides in her temple of Kâmâkhyâ[113] on the outskirts of Guwahati – and the hill of Madam Kâmâdev some forty kilometers away, where the god Kâmâ[114] resided.

Set forth below are a few verses of the *Mahâ-Kaulajñânanirnaya* in which Kâmarûpâ and Kâmâkhyâ are mentioned.

*...One should not give (knowledge) to a person who has not first been tested, but only to those who are prepared to receive it. After the initiation into the experience of **Kula**[115], one may reveal the characteristics of the essence of the Self. One should be conscious of the five jewels of **Kulâgama** [116]. The first interrupts ageing, the second gives what one desires, the third is **Kâmarûpâ**, the fourth gives immortality, and the fifth is the great jewel that destroys fever and death. (Mahâ-Kaulajñânanirnaya, Patala XVII, 11-13).*

---

[111] Kâmarûpa = Current state of Assam in northeast India which is also identified with the land of the goddess Kâmâkhya (pure consciousness).

[112] Kâmâksa = Some texts refer to the goddess Kâmâksa, and others refer to her as Kâmâkhya.

[113] Kâmâkhya = Known as enlightened awareness (Pure consciousness). A goddess represented symbolically by a stone shaped in the form of a Yoni (vulva).

[114] Kâmâ = God of love/desire.

[115] Kula = In some Tantric texts this is synonymous with Shakti (energy). Born of Shakti and Shiva. Family of Brahmans, of the Bengal lineage.

[116] Kulâgama = Agama = Tradition, Tantric texts.

*...In **Kâmarûpa**, this **Sastra** [117] is related to the **Yoginîs** that reside in each home. Those who possess this knowledge, given through grace, may use it constantly, and will be able either to favor or punish, having attained (the state) of unity by (means of) the **Yoginîs**.*

Sulocane! [118] *This great **Sastra** was revealed in **Candradvîpa** [119]. The hymns arising out of the profundities of the **Mahâmatsya** [120] were made in **Kâmâkhyâ** . (Mahâ-Kaulajñânanirnaya, Patala XXII, 8 -12).*

The temple of Kâmâkhyâ is the most well-known pîtha (sacred place) of the Devi, where her Yoni (vulva) fell while Shiva wandered across the land carrying the corpse of his wife. Shiva forgot about his divine duties and, drunk with sadness, danced about like a madman. To put an end to such behavior, Nârâyana (Vishnú) used his chariot wheel to cut the goddess' corpse into fifty-one pieces which then fell across the land and are today the fifty-one Saktipîthas where the goddess is worshipped.[121]

Shakta ideology[122] developed in eastern India in the region covered by Bengal, Orissa and Assam. One Shakta king imported Brahmans from Bengal to occupy the temple and take charge of the ceremonies in Kâmâkhyâ. At the same time, Kâmâkhyâ became one of the best-known centers of Tantra in India. Various

---

[117] Sastra = Precept, canon.

[118] Sulocane = Name which Bhairava gives to the goddess in the dialogue written in code in the Kaulajñananinaya manuscript.

[119] Candradvîpa = Birthplace of Matsyendranâtha and also where he was thrown into the sea. A great fish swallowed him and while inside the fish's belly, Matsyendranâtha overheard the dialogue between Bhairava and the Devi about how to acquire the knowledge.

[120] Mahâmatsya = A great fish.

[121] Generally at these sacred sites the goddess is worshipped in the form of a stone that symbolizes a member of her body. For example, at Siddhapura in the Katmandu Valley is a temple dedicated to the Goddess where a long stone that represents the Devi's trunk is worshipped.

[122] Shakta = Worshippers of Shakti and Shiva jointly as the union of the masculine and feminine divine energies.

sects there carry out their rites in strict secrecy; only those who have been initiated into the sect may participate.

Long lines of devotees patiently await the moment of the Darshan[123] of the sacred stone, out of which a spring arises. Other devotees at the temple's periphery offer coconuts, flowers and animals that have had their throats slit. Ambubachi[124] is the most important festival celebrated at the temple of Kâmâkhya. Between the seventh and twelfth days of the Hindu month of "Asadha" (June), the doors of the temple are closed so that the goddess may rest because she begins her menstrual cycle. When the doors again open, the instruments used in the Pûjas[125] are thoroughly washed. (Even now in India it is said symbolically that when the rains begin Mother Nature is having her menstrual cycle). Nine other temples devoted to the various representations of the Devi are situated on the hill.

Innumerable legends speak of the Kâmâkhya temple, and occasionally the themes are contradictory and chronologically inaccurate. One of them says that Kâmadeva[126] built a temple of stone dedicated to the goddess in the place where her Yoni fell, and sculptured on the walls the images of sixty-four Yoginîs and sixteen Bhairavas to accompany that symbol of the goddess. If that temple truly existed, it would be the one that was destroyed by Muslim invaders. Around the sixteenth century the temple was reconstructed on the original temple's site. It is also said that the only surviving portion of the latter was found beneath the earth, protecting the Yoni, and that the current walls are the originals.

Guwahati is an interesting city surrounded by hills next to the great Brahmaputra River. The Umananda Mandir temple is located on an island in the middle of the river which can only be reached by boat. On the river's edge is another important temple dedicated to Shiva where the faithful gather to worship a huge stone linga

---

[123] Darshan = To perceive the divine nature.
[124] Ambubachi = To converse with the water.
[125] Pujâ = A ceremony.
[126] Kâmadeva = God of love

(fallus). At the opposite end of the city is the Navagrah Mandir temple on Chitrachal Hill, also a center for astrology and astronomy.

When traveling through the humid forest that covers the undulating landscape of Assam, one feels as if transported to the era that was known as Kâmarûpa, a sensation particularly noticeable when visiting the Madan Kâmadeva site. There, savage beasts seem to lurk in the surrounding jungle, and migratory birds can be seen on the shores of the nearby lake. The ruins of statues and erotic temples from the medieval period appear among butterflies and dragonflies. The museum at the site displays sculptures which serve as mute testimony of ancient rites.

If indeed Matsyendranâtha experienced the revelation of the cult of the Yoginîs in the country of Kâmarûpa, it must have occurred in a place much like the hill of Madan Kâmadeva, where the vibrations of the ancient god Kâma linger in the air and one, if attentive, may sense the presence of the divine.

Feminie sculpture
holding a fish (Matsya)
Madam Kâmadeva Museum

17. KATHMANDU

Millions of years ago, the force of the collision between the Indian sub-continent and the Asian continent created the highest mountains on the face of the Earth: the Himalayas. Perhaps the echo caused by the impact still vibrates throughout the atmosphere. When the inhabitants of India look for the source of the sound that was the cause of creation, they turn to the north because they imagine that above the snow-capped summits the celestial sky displays the figures of the gods. Periodically, those who dwell in the heavens respond to the calls of human beings; and their first encounter with the inhabitants of the Earth took place in the valley of Kathmandu.

Nepal did not suffer the frequent Muslim invasions that wreaked havoc with part of the religious background of medieval India. Over the centuries its spiritual world was gently molded. Nepal preserved many manuscripts written in the alphabet of its vernacular languages such as Newari, as well as those originating in other places[127] where religious ideas were expressed in prayer books and poems dedicated to the Mother Goddess *Devi*, to *Shiva*, to *Vishnu* and to Buddhism. Some of these treatises are best known as *Tantra*s which offer a discourse on the nature of the Divine, as well as discussions on rites, sacred places and auspicious dates. These were written in coded languages because they were transcriptions from an oral tradition in which the Master provided the guidelines for their interpretation. They wished to differentiate them from such sacred traditional books as the *Vedas* and the

---

[127] A Thousand Year Old Bengali Mystic Poetry - Hasna Jasimuddin Moudud, Dhaka, 1992. Manuscripts of mystic poetry written in ancient Bengala and preserved in Nepal.

Upanishads, for example, which were directed to an intellectual elite. The *Tantric* texts were intended to reach the devotee through direct experience and not through intellectual analysis. The manuscripts were hidden or protected until they were forgotten, left in the abodes of followers, kings and nobles. At the beginning of the 20th century, scholars from India and Nepal were able to visit the royal libraries where they discovered these unpublished works. In the 1960s, a foundation financed by the German government and inspired by the expeditions of the great naturalist and humanist scholar Alexander von Humboldt systematically began to create a catalogue and preserve via microfilm this treasure of antique manuscripts that were discovered dispersed throughout Nepal. The name of this extraordinary organization is *The Nepal Research Centre* which has already published a number of excellent pieces. Manuscripts from the *Durbar Library* of the Nepalese royal house were taken to the National Archives where a preservation project was begun. Many of these works are written on palm leaves which are susceptible to damage from insects, weather conditions, and mildew. Fortunately, the world has become increasingly aware of the great patrimony of knowledge that these antique manuscripts represent. In India, the National Mission for Manuscripts has begun an important project that consists of linking up all the country's libraries through a common database which will facilitate research about history, philosophy, religion, and sociology. Another goal of the National Mission for Manuscripts is to develop methods to preserve palm leaves and other ancient materials used for the writing of manuscripts.

Pilgrims from the Himalayas, Tibet, India, Japan and China visit the valley of Kathmandu attracted by the abundance of rites, traditions and religious syncretism.

As for the Yoginîs, four of them are said to be in the valley. *Sankhu Vajra Yoginî* is the oldest. *Maheshvari* is for the *Shiva*-worshippers, one of the *Ashta Mâtrikâs*[128] (eight mothers). Her

---

[128] See the commentary on the Ashta Mâtrikâs in the chapter on "Two Yoginî Temples in Orissa.

iconography is identified with the known Yoginîs or with the Dakinis, but her role as a guardian can be seen by the symbols in her hands, such as a sword. The temple of *Vajra Yoginî* is located above the town of *Sankhu*, to the north-east of the valley, via an old street that leads to Helambu and Tibet. Legend has it that the Yoginî once lived in this forest and was offered bloody sacrifices. According to another Buddhist legend, the

Lord Bhairava

Vajra Yoginî's necklace of skulls was made of the heads of Brahmin followers of *Shankaracharya*[129], who were beheaded for being arrogant. The cranium-bowl containing blood offered to the Yoginî came from the fifth head of *Brahma* when he was beheaded by *Shiva-Bhairava*. At the present time blood is only offered to the image of *Bhairava* whose temple is located on the way to the temple of the Yoginî.

Sveta Matsyendranâtha

In both the Kathmandu valley and the city are innumerable temples dedicated to *Bhairava* – closely related to the cult of the *Yoginîs* – whose iconography merges with that of *Mahâkâla*, the guardian deity of the Buddhist pantheon.

Other important sites of the Kathmandu valley related to the cult of the *Yoginîs* are the temples

---

[129] Shankaracharya = Adi Shankar was the first Shankaracharya. Title given to those theologians who manage the four monasteries (maths) important to the Hindu faith.

dedicated to *Matsyendranâtha* (the deified master) to whom the ideology and rites of the cult of the *Yoginîs* is attributed. For the *Newars*[130], *Sveta*[131] *Matsyendranâtha* is *Avalokeshvara*, the *bodhisattva*[132] of compassion. He is considered to be the most important deity in Kathmandu and is venerated by all Hindus and Buddhists. On mother's day or father's day, orphans go to his temple and pay homage or simply to ask for protection. It is said that this image emanated from Buddha and that it is a *bodhisattva* that speaks to those who know how to listen, for he was blessed with the gift of speech. Every year a great festival is celebrated in honor of *Sveta Matsyendrnâtha*; the idol is paraded on a large float decorated with a long tongue whose tip bears an image of *Bhairava*. This symbolism appears to be related to the doctrine that was orally given by *Matsyendranâtha,* and which is also found hidden in *Bhairava*'s words in the *Mahâ-Khaulajñânanirnaya.*

The Rato[133] *Matsyendranâtha* is located in Patan and is also held to be the *Bodhisattva* of compassion. The legends of the master *Matsyendranâtha* intertwine with another great *Yogi*, his disciple *Gorakhnâtha* (both names are spelled in numerous ways depending on the text).

On visiting the valley of Kathmandu where several legends and cults continue to coexist, one will find a widespread interplay between the Buddhist and Tantric tendencies and the Hindu Brahman elites, influenced by the continual effect of religious syncretism.

---

[130] Newars = One of the ethnic groups of Nepal.

[131] Sveta = White

[132] Bodhisattva = Enlightened being, name given to the divine personalities of Buddhism who have temporarily or definitively renounced the state of freedom from the cycle of reincarnation. Out of pure compassion they return to Earth to aid others in attaining the state of the Buddha.

[133] Rato = Red.

MUSEUMS

For the great scholar of Eastern religions, Alexandra David-Neel, the Guimet Museum in Paris was a temple. She sought it out in search of divine inspiration. Fascinated by the serene image of Buddha represented in various sculptures, Alexandra gave herself over to the inner dialogue. She closed her eyes. She journeyed inward to the center where the images of the Great Master converged with the knowledge garnered from sacred texts. The representation of Buddha silent and absorbed in the Self took her to the light of knowledge. There, in the Guimet Museum, Alexandra David-Neel dreamed of discovering great wisdom. Years later, in her first voyage to the East, filled with emotion she sought in the temples of Sri Lanka the same ecstatic experience. But that first encounter with native Buddhism was contrary to her search and her expectations. She longed for the spiritual and intellectual experiences that she had known in the halls of the Guimet Museum and in the library. Surrounded by books, she studied, dreamed and worked.

Until the 1990s the library was still located in the central place where Alexandra and many other scholars studied and wrote about the East. The books, tables and chairs seemed to protect the emotions of those wise individuals who studied about the spiritual paths of the East. Today, the museum possesses a modern library to one side of its entrance. For those who knew the original library, all that is left is the taste of melancholy when visiting the old space surrounded by glass partitions where – like musty museum objects – some ancient tomes are displayed.

Three Yoginî sculptures in very good condition are found in the Guimet Museum, originating in southern India, from the temple that must have stood in the area near Kanchipuram.

In the West, museums have evolved. With the desire to transport the visitor to other ages and cultures. Shows create unforgettable events, and the permanent expositions are no longer content with displaying objects out of context. They have developed smart concepts of communication. The great majority of Western museums attempt to give a new dignity to the sacred object that was brutally torn from its site of worship, stripped of offerings, hymns and any hint of ceremonies and rites. The display rooms create a sophisticated sacred atmosphere through the play of wall color and between the light and shadow that illumine the sculptures exposed. The visitor approaches with caution, speaks in a low voice, reads the inscriptions, and desires to learn to distinguish and correctly name each god in order to avoid a lack of respect towards images soaked with history, legends and symbols. In front of the sculptures hurry fades and time stands still. The dialogue can be of a few seconds, or of an eternity. Without liturgies or rites, in the museums the fear of not knowing how to act or of being irreverent vanishes. The divinity there represented has transcended the ages, has traveled to its new home to acquire a new life when the eyes of the visitor gaze upon her.

In the United States, in the Denver Museum in Colorado, I witnessed the dialogue between a number of visitors and four Yoginîs that originated in Rikhiyan, sculpted in a rectangular stone block. They were exposed in a privileged site where they attracted the attention of visitors. I saw several people approach the Yoginîs, read the explanatory texts and again examine the details of the group of goddesses. When our glances crossed, there was an exchange of smiles and a whisper of words spoken at random without daring to raise our voices. This experience was repeated in other museums in North America like the Sackler Gallery of Art in Washington, D.C., the Museum of Art in Minneapolis, at the Detroit Institute of Art, the Nelson Atkings Gallery in Kansas City, and the San Antonio Museum of Art with its Yoginî from the Naresar workshop. Surely visitors will continue learning of the sacredness of the Yoginîs in the forthcoming reopening of the section for Southeast Asia at the Royal Museum of Toronto in Canada.

In Europe, in addition to the Guimet Museum in Paris, I also recommend visiting the British Museum in London where another Yoginî of the group from Kanchipuram can be found, and the Reitberg Museum in Zurich where a headless Yoginî also from Kanchipuram is displayed.

When one visits museums in India the experience is different. While silence, lighting and adequacy of space do not form part of the "rite of knowledge", the variety and quantity of the sculptures serve to make the event. I recommend visiting museums in all the cities although, at times, the objects are not well displayed and lack proper information. I particularly recommend the museums of New Delhi and Bhopal for their exhibitions and for the qualified personnel that work there; and although they display no Yoginîs, there is an extraordinary variety of sculptures and both sacred and profane images.

I found several Yoginîs from Shahdol in the museum at Dhubela. In the Archaeological Museum of Gwalior some of the Yoginîs of Naresar are displayed. In the Museum of Chennai I found one Yoginî from Kanchipuram, headless. In the Museum of Calcutta are various other Yoginîs of Shahdol. At the Birla Museum in Bhopal are four Yoginîs from Hinglajgadh; and more from there in that of Indore.

For some, museums are the temples of the modern world. The visitor enters with an intellect hungry for knowledge. Instead of revering, one analyzes the images. Instead of praying, one learns to list and classify. Instead of opening one's heart to the spiritual dialogue, one opens the intellect to catalogue the reasons behind the devotion of those others who once prostrated themselves before idols of stone or of any other material.

The variety of the diverse cultures of India is expressed in enigmatic representations of altars and goddesses that have captivated and continue to captivate the spirit and the intellect of the East and West.

The Yoginîs, far from their destroyed or forgotten temples, have found a new altar in the museums. With their expressions of strength and eternal bliss they excite the mind and change concepts. Perhaps one of these days they will begin to fly until they find their multiple facets dispersed around the world; and with their invisible wings they will shake away prejudices and awaken minds and hearts to new perspectives.

ITINERARIES

Seven to ten days

Temple	Accommodation site	Approximate distance
1. Hirapur	Bhubaneshwar	15 km.
	Balangir	385 km.
2. Ranipur Jharial		104 km.
	Raipur	180 km.
	Amarkantak	235 km.
3. Bheraghat	Bheraghat	240 km.

The best way to visit the Yoginî temples is by private car or taxi because the temples are generally located in remote areas where public transportation is not available. On interstate highways, it is possible to drive at 60 kilometers per hour but on secondary roads the average speed is usually about 30 kilometers per hour, because these roads are often in bad shape due to the torrential rains of the monsoon season that erode them year after year.

Having the most recent maps of Orissa, Uttar Pradesh and Madhya Pradesh is a requirement. But even if not up-to-date, they will still be useful for calculating distances. Differences between a map and the actual situation are generally due to the fact that the secondary roads have become main arteries over time. They may also be due to new routes not being included, but in any event the original roads will not vanish from the maps.

It is also advisable to carry a compass. It will be particularly useful at crossroads.

Lacking a private vehicle, one may choose to hire a taxi for several days. Fares per day are calculated by the kilometer and vary depending on the size of the car and on features such as air conditioning availability. One should prepared to pay for a minimum of 200 to 300[134] kilometers (whether or not they are actually traveled). Every travel agency has their own criteria but must of them calculate in terms of 250km per day.

1. Hirapur. There are direct flights from Delhi, Mumbai (Bombay), Kolkata (Calcutta) and Chennai (Madras) to Bhubaneshwar- capital of Orissa's state — and the nearest city to approach Hirapur. The railway and the interstate highway that connect Kolkata and Chennai go through the coastal rout of Orissa. The railway and the roads coming from the Madhya Pradesh and Chhattisgarh States arrive to Bhubaneshwar.

Three to four days are required to visit Bhubaneshwar and its surroundings. The first day should be reserved for the impressive quantity of temples from the city. It is also worth to save one whole day to visit the temple dedicated to the Sun God Surya in Konark and to discover the holy city of Puri on the seashore, not to far from Konark.

You can find guide and art books at the many books-shops in Bhubaneshwar that would explain the temples and give information about the Udayagiri and Khandhagiri caves[135]. Travel agencies and drivers in Bhubaneshwar know the route to Hirapur even though they don't propose the visit in their brochures.

The best time of the year to visit Orissa state is between October and February. The temperature in December can go as low as 15°C and reaches its maximum of about 48°C in May.

2. Ranipur Jharial. It is important to consult a current map of Orissa for this visit.

At least two days are needed to visit the Ranipur Jharial temple, whether ones arrives from Bhubaneshwar or from Raipur, the capital city of the neighboring state of Chhattisgarh.

Leaving from Bhubaneshwar by auto, one travels through countryside where lovely rural temples adorn the route. It is advisable to spend the night in Balangir, 104 kilometers from

---

[134] For your own safety do not ask your driver to do more than 300km per day.

[135] Jain caves on the way to Hirapur.

Ranipur Jharial. Balangir, capital city of the district by the same name, is not a city with a well-developed tourist industry and only has two or three hotels.

The journey is colorful. In India's rural areas the peasants open their doors to visitors, allowing them to share in the peasants' daily routine. Life occurs mostly outdoors during the daytime; and even in the hottest months of the year people sleep outside. Mothers can be seen bathing their children at roadside water stands, or washing their household items. Peasant women in colorful saris and their erect posture become elegant queens even while performing such domestic chores as carrying water or pots. They can be seen hanging clothes on roofs or on any other surface to dry under the sun, while children play happily with simple toys probably made by their parents. At times one may quietly witness the process of planting in which, shoulder-to-shoulder, men and women walk the fields sowing the seeds. The images move to the slow rhythm of the sun crossing the sky.

The trip between Raipur and Amarkantak will take between 8 and 9 hours in a private car. (At an average speed of 30 kilometers per hour on secondary roads or when transiting forest reserves, such as the one in Achanakmar.) One may also reach Amarkantak by bus from Raipur, Shahdol or Jabalpur.

Amarkantak, situated at the source of the Narmada River, was the religious inspiration of the Nâthas[136] and an important center of the Tantric religion. It is considered the home of the Matsyendranâtha cult. It is particularly sacred because it is the origin of the Narmada River whose waters run toward the west, in a direction opposite to the other major Indian rivers. Legend tells that Shiva blessed the waters of the Narmada with healing powers capable of liberating the soul from its bonds and burdens. It is well known in India that to purify himself the devotee must dive into the Ganges, or pray for seven days on the shore of the Yamuna or three days beside the Saraswati, but need only briefly view the Narmada in order to obtain similar results.

---

[136] Pious men devoted to Shiva; spiritual men from different confessions have this title too. (Jain, Vaishna, etc.)

4. Bheraghat is a place of pilgrimage. Devotees go there to bathe in the Narmada River. Bheraghat has many well-known hotels, simple but clean. The town is close to the domestic airport of Jabalpur.

Two-week Itinerary

Temple	Accommodation site	Approximate distance
1. Hirapur	Bhubaneshwar	15 km.
	Balangir	385 km.
2. Ranipur Jharial		104 km.
	Raipur	180 km.
	Amarkantak	235 km.
4. Bheraghat	Bheraghat	240 km.
5. Khajuraho	Khajuraho	300 km.
	Gwalior	285 km.
8. Mitauli	Gwalior	35 km.

5. Khajuraho: The distance from Bheraghat to Khajuraho is approximately 300 kilometers. Although the trip is long, it can be done in one day. It can also be done in two days if one wishes to stop at the Pana game reserve where a few tigers can be seen. Hotels in the reserve are much more expensive than those in Khajuraho.

The distance from Khajuraho to Gwalior is about 285 kilometers. The trip can be done in two steps, by spending one night in the picturesque historical city of Orchha. This stopover is also convenient if one wishes to visit the museum in Dhubela, where the Yoginî sculptures from the two Shahdol temples can be found. It is also possible to reach Gwalior by plane from Delhi.

8. Mitauli: The Mitauli temple is located in the Morena district. There are two ways to get there. The first leads from the main road that connects Morena and Gwalior. Some 11 kilometers beyond Morena (23 before Gwalior) one passes a village called Tekri just before crossing the Nurabad River. Turn left there at a secondary road. Further down the road crosses a railway line that runs between Chhattisgarh and Amritsar. Driving slowly

looking north, one will see in the midst of the countryside the stony mountain on whose peak sits the Mitauli temple.

Heading East, Mitauli can also be reached from Gwalior, by taking the road that goes to the Gohard Road, (road 92). About 22 kilometers from Gwalior is the Malanpur industrial area; from there, one follows the road that leads through the fields to the Morena-Gwalior main road. Further west, after passing a small road sign indicating a Vishnu temple, the sign post for the Padhauli site appears at one side of the road and the other side is the one for Mitauli. Blending with the peak of the stony summit, the Mitauli temple appears on the horizon. At the foot of the hill where the temple is located, a sign describes the site as a Mahadev lingas temple, making no mention to the Yoginîs.

Three-week Itinerary

Temple	Accommodation Site	Distance
1. Hirapur	Bhubaneshwar	15 km.
	Balangir	385 km.
2. Ranipur Jharial		104 km.
	Raipur	180 km.
	Amarkantak	235 km.
3. Shahdol	Jabalpur or Bheraghat	350 km.
4. Bheraghat	Bheraghat (near Jabalpur)	
5. Khajuraho	Khajuraho	300 km.
	Dhubela Museum and Mau-Suhania	45 km.
	Orccha-Lalitpur	130 km. + 100 km.
6. Dudahi	Lalitpur	15 km. + 5 km. walking
7. Badoh	Lalitpur	35 km.
	Gwalior	200 km.
8. Mitauli	Gwalior	35 km.
9. Naresar	Gwalior	30 km.
	Orccha	100 km.
	Chitrakoot	300 km.
	Rypura, on the road to Mau	10 km.
10. Lokhari		15 km.
11. Rikhiyan	from Mau	25 km. + 17 km.
	Fortress of Garwha - Allahabad	50 km.
12. Varanasi	Varanasi	80 km.

108

3. Shahdol: The detour to Shahdol off the route from Amarkantak to Bheraghat probably takes a hundred kilometers of travel. Dr. Dehejia commented in her 1986 book Yoginî Cult that only a few Yoginî sculptures in very bad condition were to be found in the temples of small villages in the Shahdol district (Antara and Panchgaon).

5. Khajuraho: (See the first section on Khajuraho in the Two-Week Itinerary, above). **Dhubela museum and Mau-Suhania temple:** In the museum of Dhubela located some 50 kilometers from Khajuraho are 20 sculptures that belonged to two temples from the Shahdol district. Dr. Devangana Desai wrote in her book The Religious Imagery of Khajuraho that close to the Dhubela museum, in Mau-Suhania in the Chhatarpur district, she observed the ruins of twenty-four niches placed around a rectangular courtyard open to the sky. These are probably the ruins of another temple dedicated to the Yoginîs.

Orccha-Lalitpur: Orccha is an interesting tourist site with many different kinds of hotels; however, due to the distance between Orccha and Dudahi it is better to stay in Lalitpur, 100 kilometers from Orccha. The only inconvenience is that Lalitpur lacks good hotels for tourists.

6. Dudahi: Passing the Lalitpur area, skirt the Govinda Sagar Lake and continue south. You will pass an Uttar Pradesh control station but there is yet a long way to the border. About 10 kilometres past the control station, take a road to the west toward Pali. From the plain along this road a few hills can be seen. One of the small roads leads to the town of Dudhai, which pertains to the district of Lalitpur. During the rainy season, the town appears as if it stands on the shore of a large pond. The rest of the year the pond is filled with crops. Passing through the town, two kilometres on foot or by tractor, is the small hill crowned by a round temple. The townspeople and those of the area call it Akhada, as they call places where soldiers practice wrestling. The ruins of the religious centre of Dudhai consist of two areas: one with the Yoginî temple and the other contains the ruins of temples dedicated to Brahma, Shiva, Vishnu and Jain saints.

7. Badoh: Sixty kilometers from Lalitpur on the road to Sagar, after the town of Barodia, one can take the road towards Khurai and from there to Phatari (because Badoh and Phatari were once just a single town). Today there are practically no remnants of what was said to be the Yoginî temple. Of the forty-two niches where the Yoginîs supposedly were, only a few traces now remain of the cells that probably surrounded a rectangular stone platform. What exists now is the temple called Gardamal of the mothers.

Lalitpur – Gwalior: After the detour to visit the Dudahi and Badoh temples, one will have to spend the night again at Lalitpur in order to complete the long journey of approximately 200 kilometers to Gwalior the following day.

9. Naresar: Thirty kilometers north of Gwalior, the road crosses a lonely plain and leads to the shelters of nomad shepherds at the base of a stony peak. After about a two kilometer walk one reaches Naresar. There lie the ruins of a pond along with a number of preserved temples.

Orccha, Chitrakoot: The road between Gwalior and Chitrakoot is long. Depending on how willing one is to look for accommodations in a number of small towns on the road, it is preferable to spend the night in Orccha. Chitrakoot is a pilgrimage center, a holy city on the shores of the Narmada River. It is said that the gods were born there, and that Rama was exiled there along with his brother and Sita. It is a border town between Madhya Pradesh and Uttar Pradesh. There are guesthouses in both states where one can find good food and fully equipped rooms.

Rypura: From Chitrakoot, traveling the road that leads to Allahabad and before reaching Mau, one finds a village called Rypura. There, in the police station is located one of the Yoginîs of Lokhari. This is the only sculpture that was saved from the thieves who stole one-by-one the precious images which for many years were abandoned in Lokhari. The police have constructed a small temple to shelter the Yoginî and describe on a metal plate the story of its rescue. They gave the Yoginî the name of Kalikâ, but Dr. Dehejia identified her as Rksânanâ (the bear-faced Yoginî).

110

10. Lokhari: One reaches Lokhari by following the road to Mau. Arriving at Lalta Road, in the middle of the town one takes the road to the right and follows it to arrive at Lokhari village. On one side can be seen the ruins of a large fortress which is not accessible from that point. A stairway invites one to climb to the summit of another stone hill where even yet lie the remains of various sculptures. It seems that the thieves broke many while transporting the Yoginîs, or the policemen caused the damage while trying to save them. The rest are found in the Garwha fortress, 50 kilometers from Allahabad.

11. Rikhiyan: The local pronunciation is Rishian, which probably refers to the window of the Rishis. In the middle of the town of Mau, one takes the road to the left. This little road borders the Jamuna River, often hidden behind the overgrowth. After traveling about 17 kilometers one reaches a water pump next to a small Durga shrine. On the river side of the road are the ruins of several temples. On the other side, among cultivated fields is a path that can be followed only on foot, and which leads to some caves. In the darkness of the caves are erect lingas within their respective yonis. People say that the caves once connected to Chitrakoot. Among the ruins of the temples dedicated to Shiva are no temples dedicated to the Devi, nor the ruins of any rectangular sanctuary dedicated to the Yoginîs. It is supposed that the Rikhiyan temple must have been rectangular because the Yoginîs are sculpted – in groups of four – on rectangular blocks of stone. In the silent and deserted landscape next to the pond are stony heights where the Rikhian temple was probably located.

The Fortress of Garwha (Gadhwa): Continuing along the road from Mau to Allahabad, the Garwha fortress is located about 50 kilometers prior to reaching Allahabad. Various temples are protected there. In a warehouse behind a fence are the panels of the Rikhiyan Yoginîs piled among the remains of a few Yoginîs from Lokhari.

12. Varanasi: The sacred city of Varanasi is about 80 kilometers from Allahabad. There is a temple located there called

Chousatti Devi (sixty-four Devis). As its name implies, the current building was probably erected on the same site where a temple dedicated to the sixty-four Yoginîs once stood. From the fact that its name appears in ancient philosophic and religious treaties, Varanasi has been known for more than 2,000 years. But the city was destroyed many times. The oldest buildings are only two hundred years old. It is very likely that centuries ago Varanasi was not so spread out. It is therefore possible that a temple to the sixty-four Yoginîs stood at Chausati Ghat and would have, at that time, been located far from what was then the center of Varanasi. That temple may have been either circular or rectangular in shape. It has been seen that temples dedicated to Yoginîs were built in isolated places, but always near a city where religious activities took place or where patrons lived who were often royalty.

Full Itinerary

Temple	Accommodation Site	Distance
1. Hirapur	Bhubaneshwar	15 km.
	Balangir	385 km.
2. Ranipur Jharial		104 km.
	Raipur*	180 km.
	Amarkantak	235 km.
3. Shahdol	Jabalpur* or Bheraghat	350 km.
4. Bheraghat	Bheraghat (near Jabalpur)	5. Khajuraho
Khajuraho*		300 km.
	Dhubela Museum and Mau	45 km.
	Orccha-Lalitpur	130 km. +100 km.
6. Dudahi	Lalitpur	15 km. + 5 km. walking
7. Badoh	Lalitpur	35 km.
	Gwalior*	200 km.
8. Mitauli	Gwalior	35 km.
9. Naresar	Gwalior	30 km.
	Orccha	100 km.
	Chitrakoot	300 km.
Rypura - Mau		10 km.
10. Lokhari		15 km.
11. Rikhiyan		25 km. + 17 km.
from Mau		

Garwha Fort-   50 km.
Allahabad
12. Varanasi   Varanasi*   80 km.
13. Hinglajgadh   Via Jaipur*or Bhopal*, overnight in Jhalawar
14. Kanchipuram   Chennai*
15. Delhi   Delhi*
16.Guwahati   Guwahati*
17.Kathmandú   Kathmandu*
* Served by airports

13. Hinglajgadh: One can reach Hinglajgadh via Jaipur (the capital of Rajasthan) or Bhopal (in Madhya Pradesh). The closest city is Jhalawar (in Rajasthan), a small historically interesting city. Nowadays at Hinglajgadh one can only find the ruins of a fortress that was presumably constructed after the temple of the Yoginîs. The Yoginî sculptures found at Hinglajgadh are now housed at the Birla Museum in Bhopal.

14. Kanchipuram: Chennai (Madras) is the closest airport to Kanchipuram. There is no trace of the location of the temple dedicated to the Kanchipuram Yoginîs, which are today found in many museums throughout Europe and North America. There is only one headless sculpture in the museum of Chennai. According to Dr. Dehejia the sculptures are similar to others found in Kaveripakkan, in northwestern Kanchipuram. Today no iconography in the style of "Yoginîs of Kanchipuram" is recognized in either Kaveripakkan or Kanchipuram.

15. Delhi: Known in ancient times as Yoginipûra (City of the Yoginîs).

16. Guwahati: Kâmarûpa is related to the current state of Assam whose capital is Guwahati and where an important temple dedicated to the Devi is located. It is said that Kâmarûpa was where Matsyendranâtha – the great Yoga master – had his revelation concerning the cult of the Yoginîs.

17. Kathmandu: In the Katmandu Valley are two temples dedicated to Matsyendrnâtha. During medieval times, the mysticism of Katmandu attracted great thinkers who left their legacy of esoteric knowledge in manuscripts that are now found solely in state and private libraries. Only at the beginning of the 20th century did some historians and experts begin to have access to these manuscripts. The study of the knowledge preserved in Nepal is only just beginning to be known. Some manuscripts speak of the mysticism of the cult of the Yoginîs.

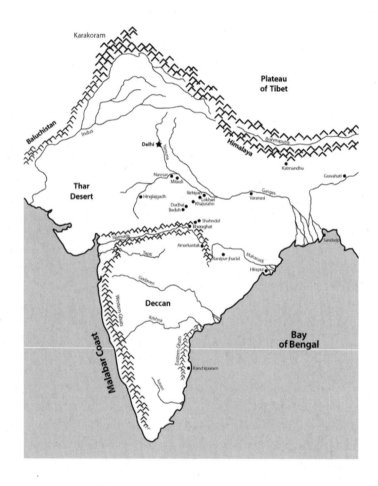

Yogini Sites and Temples
Sketch map of the Indian Subcontinent

Museums in India
Dhubela Museum: Yoginîs from Shahdol
Archaeological Museum of Gwalior: Yoginîs from Naresar
Museum of Chennai*: Yoginî from Kanchipuram
Museum of Calcutta*: Yoginîs from Shahdol
Museum of Birla in Bhopal*: Yoginîs from Hinglajgadh
Museum of Indore: Yoginîs from Hinglajgadh

International Museums
Musée Guimet de Paris: Yoginîs from Kanchipuram
Bristish Museum in London: Yoginî from Kanchipuram
Reitberg Museum in Zurich: Yoginî from Kanchipuâm
Royal Ontario Museum in Toronto: Yoginî from Kanchipuram
The Minneapolis Museum of Arts in Mineapolis: Yoginî from Kanchipuram
The Detroit Institue of Arts in Detroit: Yoginî from Kanchipuram (in Dr. Vidya Dehejia's book it is labelled as Yoginî from Kaverippankam)
The Sackler Gallery of Arts in Washington D.C.: Yoginî from Kanchipuram
The Nelson Atkings Gallery in Kansas City: Yoginî from Kanchipuram
Denver Art Museum: Yoginîs from Rikhiyan
Fowler Museum in Los Angeles: Yoginî from Mitauli
Boston Museum of Fine Arts (Shiva playing music, same style as that of the Yoginîs from Kanchipuram)
The San Antonio Museum of Art, Yoginî from Naresar's workshop.

SELECT BIBLIOGRAPHY

DEHEJIA, Vidya, *Yoginî Cult and Temples, A Tantric Tradition,* National Museum, Janpath, New Delhi, 1986

DEHEJIA, Vidya, *Early Stone Temples of Orissa,* Carolina Academic Press, Durham, 1979

DEHEJIA, Vidya, Devi, The Great Goddess, Arthur M. Sackler Gallery, Smithsonian Institution, Washington, D.C., 1999

DESAI, Devangana, *The religious Imagery of Khajuraho,* Project for Indian Cultural Studies, Publication IV, Mumbai 1996

DESAI, Devangana, *Erotic Sculpture of India, A Socio-Cultural Study,* Tata McGraw-Hill Publishing Co., New Delhi

DYCZKOWSKI, Mark, The Cult of Godess Kubjikâ, *A preliminary Comparative Textual and Antropological Survey of Secret Newar Godess,* Franz Steiner Verlag, Stuttgart 2001

DYCZKOWSKI, Mark, *A journey in the World of the Tantras,* Indica Books, Varanasi, 2004

DYCZKOWSKI, Mark, *The Canon of the Saivagâma and the Kubjikâ Tantras of the Western Kuala Tradition,* Delhi, 1989

GORDON WHITE, David, *The Kiss of the Yoginî,* The University of Chicago Press, Chicago and London, 2003

GORDON WHITE, David, *The Alchemical Body, Siddha Traditions in Medieval India,* The University of Chicago Press, Chicago and London, 1996

Select Bibliography

ELIADE, Mircea, *Briser le Toit de la Maison, La Créativité et ses Symbolées*, Gallimard, Paris, 1986

ELIADE, Mircea, *Le Yoga, Immortalité et liberté*, Payot, Paris, 1983

ELIADE, Mircea, *Patanjali et le Yoga*, Edition du Seuil, Paris 1962

ELIADE, Mircea, *Le sacré et le Profane*, Gallimard, Paris, 1965

ELIADE, Mircea, *Mito y realidad (Aspects du mythe)*, Barcelona 1991

MATSYENDRANATHA, de su escuela, *Mâhakaulajñânanirnaya*, manuscrito en hojas de palma, siglo XI (?)

BAGCHI, P.C., *Kaulajñânanirnaya and some minor texts of the school of Matsyendranâtha*, Calcutta, 1934

BAGCHI, P.C., *Tantra Granthamala No. 12, Kaulanananirnaya of the School of Matsyendranatha*, Varanasi, 1986

AVALON, Arthur, (WOODROFFE, Sir John) *Kulârnava Tantra*, Delhi, 2000

AVALON, Arthur, (WOODROFFE, Sir John) *The garland of letters*, Madras 1974

BANDYOPADHYAY, Pranab, *The Goddess of Tantra*, Calcutta 1990

CHAKRABORTI, Haripada, *Sâkta Tântrik Cult in India*, Calcutta 1996

DAS, H.C., *Iconography of Sâkta Divinities*, Delhi 1997

HAQUE, Emanuel, *Bengal Sculptures, Hindu Iconography upto c.1250 A.D.*, Bangladesh National Museum, Dhaka, 1992

JUNG, L'homme et ses symbols, Paris 1964

KAIMAL, Padma, *Seductive,* Rotunda-2- Summer Fall 2003, The ROM, Toronto

KAIMAL, Padma, *Learning to See the Goddess Once Again: Male and female in Balance at the Kailâsanâth Temple in Kânchipuram,* Journal of Academy of Religion, March 2005, Vol. 73, No 1, pp. 45-87

KARAMBELKAR, V.W., *Matsyendrnath and his Yogini Cult*, Indian Historical Quartely XXXI: 362-374, 1985

KARAMBELKAR, V.W., *Magic Ritual in Sanskrit Fiction*, Journal Ganganath Jha Institute, Allahabad, VII: 125-141

KUMAR SHARMA, Dr., Pushpendra, *Sakti and Her Episodes*, Delhi 1997

KUMAR, Suphal, *Delhi City of Yoginis*, Pilgrims Publishing, Varanasi 2006

FABRI, Charles L., History of the Art of Orissa, Calcutta, 1984

de MALLMANN, Marie Thérèse, Les enseignements iconographiques de l'Agni Purana, Paris, 1963, Annales du Musee Guimet Bibliotheque d' Etudes-Vol.LXVII

MOUDUD, Hasna Jasimuddin, *A Thousand Year Old Bengali Mystic Poetry*, Dhaka, 1992

NAGAR, Shantilal, *Yoginî Shrines and Saktapîthas,* Delhi, 2006

PAL, Pratapaditya, ed., *Orissa Revisited*, Mumbai, 2001

SANTIDEVA, Sadhu, Encyclopedia of Tantra, Delhi 1999

SING, Jaideva, *Vijñaânabhairava, or Divine Conciousness*, Delhi 2003

SHASTRI, Biswanarayan, ed. *Kâlikâpurâne Mûrtivinirdesah*, Indira Gandhi National Centre of Arts, Delhi 1994

TUCCI, Giuseppe, The Theory and Practice of Mandala, London 1971

i VEDAVYAS, K.D., Skanda Purana, Calcutta, 1965

EXTRAITS OF MANUSCRIPTS, *Mahâ- Kaulajñânanirnaya, Srî Matottara Tantra, Kulârnava Tantra,*

www.pilgrimsbooks.com

**For more details, Please Visit-
www.pilgrimsbooks.com
or
for Mail Order and Catalogue
contact us at**

PILGRIMS BOOK HOUSE
B. 27/98 A-8 Nawab Ganj Road
Durga Kund Varanasi 221010
Tel: 91-542-2314060
Fax: 91-542-2312456
E-mail: pilgrimsbooks@sify.com

PILGRIMS BOOK HOUSE (New Delhi)
2391, Tilak Street, Chuna Mandi, Paharganj,
New Delhi 110055
Tel: 91-11-23584015, 23584839
Fax: 91-11-23584019
E-mail: pilgrim@del2.vsnl.net.in
E-mail: pilgrimsinde@gmail.com

PILGRIMS BOOK HOUSE (Kathmandu)
P O Box 3872, Thamel, Kathmandu, Nepal
Tel: 977-1-4700942
Off: 977-1-4700919
Fax: 977-1-4700943
E-mail: pilgrims@wlink.com.np